Praxis II

Citizenship Education:
Content Knowledge (5087) Exam

SECRETS

Study Guide
Your Key to Exam Success

agglomeration

Praxis II Test Review for the
Praxis II: Subject Assessments

Dear Future Exam Success Story:

Congratulations on your purchase of our study guide. Our goal in writing our study guide was to cover the content on the test, as well as provide insight into typical test taking mistakes and how to overcome them.

Standardized tests are a key component of being successful, which only increases the importance of doing well in the high-pressure high-stakes environment of test day. How well you do on this test will have a significant impact on your future, and we have the research and practical advice to help you execute on test day.

The product you're reading now is designed to exploit weaknesses in the test itself, and help you avoid the most common errors test takers frequently make.

How to use this study guide

We don't want to waste your time. Our study guide is fast-paced and fluff-free. We suggest going through it a number of times, as repetition is an important part of learning new information and concepts.

First, read through the study guide completely to get a feel for the content and organization. Read the general success strategies first, and then proceed to the content sections. Each tip has been carefully selected for its effectiveness.

Second, read through the study guide again, and take notes in the margins and highlight those sections where you may have a particular weakness.

Finally, bring the manual with you on test day and study it before the exam begins.

Your success is our success

We would be delighted to hear about your success. Send us an email and tell us your story. Thanks for your business and we wish you continued success.

Sincerely,

Mometrix Test Preparation Team

Need more help? Check out our flashcards at: http://MometrixFlashcards.com/PraxisII

TABLE OF CONTENTS

Top 20 Test Taking Tips

1. Carefully follow all the test registration procedures
2. Know the test directions, duration, topics, question types, how many questions
3. Setup a flexible study schedule at least 3-4 weeks before test day
4. Study during the time of day you are most alert, relaxed, and stress free
5. Maximize your learning style; visual learner use visual study aids, auditory learner use auditory study aids
6. Focus on your weakest knowledge base
7. Find a study partner to review with and help clarify questions
8. Practice, practice, practice
9. Get a good night's sleep; don't try to cram the night before the test
10. Eat a well balanced meal
11. Know the exact physical location of the testing site; drive the route to the site prior to test day
12. Bring a set of ear plugs; the testing center could be noisy
13. Wear comfortable, loose fitting, layered clothing to the testing center; prepare for it to be either cold or hot during the test
14. Bring at least 2 current forms of ID to the testing center
15. Arrive to the test early; be prepared to wait and be patient
16. Eliminate the obviously wrong answer choices, then guess the first remaining choice
17. Pace yourself; don't rush, but keep working and move on if you get stuck
18. Maintain a positive attitude even if the test is going poorly
19. Keep your first answer unless you are positive it is wrong
20. Check your work, don't make a careless mistake

United States History

Well-known Native Americans

The following are five well-known Native Americans and their roles in early US history:
- Squanto, an Algonquian, helped early English settlers survive the hard winter by teaching them the native methods of planting corn, squash, and pumpkins.
- Pocahontas, also Algonquian, became famous as a liaison with John Smith's Jamestown colony in 1607.
- Sacagawea, a Shoshone, served a vital role in the Lewis and Clark expedition when the two explorers hired her as their guide in 1805.
- Crazy Horse and Sitting Bull led Sioux and Cheyenne troops in the Battle of the Little Bighorn in 1876, soundly defeating George Armstrong Custer.
- Chief Joseph, a leader of the Nez Perce who supported peaceful interaction with white settlers, attempted to relocate his tribe to Canada rather than move them to a reservation.

Native American groups

The major regional Native American groups and the major traits of each are as follows:
- The Algonquians in the eastern part of the United States lived in wigwams. The northern tribes subsisted on hunting and gathering, while those who were farther south grew crops such as corn.
- The Iroquois, also an east coast tribe, spoke a different language from the Algonquians, and lived in rectangular longhouses.
- The Plains tribes lived between the Mississippi River and the Rocky Mountains. These nomadic tribes lived in teepees and followed the buffalo herds. Plains tribes included the Sioux, Cheyenne, Comanche and Blackfoot.
- Pueblo tribes included the Zuni, Hopi, and Acoma. They lived in the Southwest deserts in homes made of stone or adobe. They domesticated animals and cultivated corn and beans.
- On the Pacific coast, tribes such as the Tlingit, Chinook and Salish lived on fish as well as deer, native berries and roots. Their rectangular homes housed large family groups, and they used totem poles.
- In the far north, the Aleuts and Inuit lived in skin tents or igloos. Talented fishermen, they built kayaks and umiaks and also hunted caribou, seals, whales and walrus.

Age of Exploration

The Age of Exploration is also called the Age of Discovery. It is generally considered to have begun in the early fifteenth century and continued into the seventeenth century. Major developments of the Age of Exploration included technological advances in navigation, mapmaking and shipbuilding. These advances led to expanded European exploration of the rest of the world. Explorers set out from several European countries, including Portugal,

Spain, France and England, seeking new routes to Asia. These efforts led to the discovery of new lands, as well as colonization in India, Asia, Africa, and North America.

> ➤ **Review Video:** Age of Exploration
> *Visit **mometrix.com/academy** and enter **Code**: **167264***

Advancements in navigation and seafaring tools

For long ocean journeys, it was important for sailors to be able to find their way home even when their vessels sailed far out to sea. A variety of navigational tools enabled them to launch ambitious journeys over long distances. The compass and astrolabe were particularly important advancements. The magnetic compass was used by Chinese navigators from approximately 200 B.C.E., and knowledge of the astrolabe came to Europe from Arab navigators and traders who had refined designs developed by the ancient Greeks. The Portuguese developed a ship called a caravel in the 1400s that incorporated navigational advancements with the ability to make long sea journeys. Equipped with this advanced vessel, the Portuguese achieved a major goal of the Age of Exploration by discovering a sea route from Europe to Asia in 1498.

Voyage of Christopher Columbus

In 1492, Columbus, a Genoan explorer, obtained financial backing from King Ferdinand and Queen Isabella of Spain to seek a sea route to Asia. He sought a trade route with the Asian Indies to the west. With three ships, the *Niña*, the *Pinta* and the *Santa Maria*, he eventually landed in the West Indies. While Columbus failed in his effort to discover a western route to Asia, he is credited with the discovery of the Americas.

> ➤ **Review Video:** Chistopher Columbus
> *Visit **mometrix.com/academy** and enter **Code**: **765231***

Colonization of the Americas

France, Spain, the Netherlands, and England each had specific goals in the colonization of the Americas:
- Initial French colonies were focused on expanding the fur trade. Later, French colonization led to the growth of plantations in Louisiana which brought numerous African slaves to the New World.
- Spanish colonists came to look for wealth, and to convert the natives to Christianity. For some, the desire for gold led to mining in the New World, while others established large ranches.
- The Dutch were also involved in the fur trade, and imported slaves as the need for laborers increased.
- British colonists arrived with various goals. Some were simply looking for additional income, while others were fleeing Britain to escape religious persecution.

New England colonies
The New England colonies were New Hampshire, Connecticut, Rhode Island and Massachusetts. These colonies were founded largely to escape religious persecution in England. The beliefs of the Puritans, who migrated to America in the 1600s, significantly

influenced the development of these colonies. Situated in the northeast coastal areas of America, the New England colonies featured numerous harbors as well as dense forests. The soil, however, was rocky and had a very short growing season, so was not well suited for agriculture. The economy of New England during the colonial period centered around fishing, shipbuilding and trade along with some small farms and lumber mills. Although some groups congregated in small farms, life centered mainly in towns and cities where merchants largely controlled the trade economy. Coastal cities such as Boston grew and thrived.

Middle or Middle Atlantic Colonies

The Middle or Middle Atlantic Colonies were New York, New Jersey, Pennsylvania and Delaware. Unlike the New England colonies, where most colonists were from England and Scotland, the Middle Colonies founders were from various countries including the Netherlands and Sweden. Various factors led these colonists to America. More fertile than New England, the Middle Colonies became major producers of crops including rye, oats, potatoes, wheat, and barley. Some particularly wealthy inhabitants owned large farms and/or businesses. Farmers in general were able to produce enough to have a surplus to sell. Tenant farmers also rented land from larger land owners.

Southern Colonies

The Southern Colonies were Maryland, Virginia, North Carolina, South Carolina and Georgia. Of the Southern Colonies, Virginia was the first permanent English colony and Georgia the last. The warm climate and rich soil of the south encouraged agriculture, and the growing season was long. As a result, economy in the south was based largely on labor-intensive plantations. Crops included tobacco, rice and indigo, all of which became valuable cash crops. Most land in the south was controlled by wealthy plantation owners and farmers. Labor on the farms came in the form of indentured servants and African slaves. The first of these African slaves arrived in Virginia in 1619.

French and Indian Wars

The British defeat of the Spanish Armada in 1588 led to the decline of Spanish power in Europe. This in turn led the British and French into battle several times between 1689 and 1748. These wars were:
- King William's War, or the Nine Years War, 1689-1697. This war was fought largely in Flanders.
- The War of Spanish Succession, or Queen Anne's War, 1702-1713
- War of Austrian Succession, or King George's War, 1740-1748

The fourth and final war, the French and Indian War (1754-1763), was fought largely in the North American territory, and resulted in the end of France's reign as a colonial power in North America. Although the French held many advantages, including more cooperative colonists and numerous Indian allies, the strong leadership of William Pitt eventually led the British to victory. Costs incurred during the wars eventually led to discontent in the colonies and helped spark the American Revolution.

Navigation Acts

The Navigation Acts, enacted in 1651, were an attempt by Britain to dominate international trade. Aimed largely at the Dutch, the Acts banned foreign ships from transporting goods to the British colonies, and from transporting goods to Britain from elsewhere in Europe. While the restrictions on trade angered some colonists, these Acts were helpful to other American colonists who, as members of the British Empire, were legally able to provide ships for Britain's growing trade interests and use the ships for their own trading ventures. By the time the French and Indian War had ended, one-third of British merchant ships were built in the American colonies. Many colonists amassed fortunes in the shipbuilding trade.

Higher taxes after the French and Indian War

The French and Indian War created circumstances for which the British desperately needed more revenue. These needs included:
- Paying off the war debt
- Defending the expanding empire
- Governing Britain's 33 far-flung colonies, including the American colonies

To meet these needs, the British passed additional laws, increasing revenues from the colonies. Because they had spent so much money to defend the American colonies, the British felt it was appropriate to collect considerably higher taxes from them. The colonists felt this was unfair, and many were led to protest the increasing taxes. Eventually, protest led to violence.

Triangular trade

Triangular trade began in the Colonies with ships setting off for Africa, carrying rum. In Africa, the rum was traded for gold or slaves. Ships then went from Africa to the West Indies, trading slaves for sugar, molasses, or money. To complete the triangle, the ships returned to the colonies with sugar or molasses to make more rum, as well as stores of gold and silver. This trade triangle violated the Molasses Act of 1733, which required the colonists to pay high duties to Britain on molasses acquired from French, Dutch, and Spanish colonies. The colonists ignored these duties, and the British government adopted a policy of salutary neglect by not enforcing them.

Effects of new laws on British-Colonial relations

While earlier revenue-generating acts such as the Navigation Acts brought money to the colonists, the new laws after 1763 required colonists to pay money back to Britain. The British felt this was fair since the colonists were British subjects and since they had incurred debt protecting the Colonies. The colonists felt it was not only unfair, but illegal.

The development of local government in America had given the colonists a different view of the structure and role of government. This made it difficult for the British to understand the colonists' protests against what the British felt was a fair and reasonable solution to the mother country's financial problems.

Increasing discontent in the American colonies

More and more colonists were born on American soil, decreasing any sense of kinship with the far away British rulers. Their new environment had led to new ideas of government and a strong view of the colonies as a separate entity from Britain. Colonists were allowed to self-govern in domestic issues, but Britain controlled international issues. In fact, the

American colonies were largely left to form their own local government bodies, giving them more freedom than any other colonial territory. This gave the colonists a sense of independence, which led them to resent control from Britain. Threats during the French and Indian War led the colonists to call for unification in order to protect themselves.

Difference between colonial government and British government

As new towns and other legislative districts developed in America, the colonists began to practice representative government. Colonial legislative bodies were made up of elected representatives chosen by male property owners in the districts. These individuals represented the interests of the districts from which they had been elected. By contrast, in Britain the Parliament represented the entire country. Parliament was not elected to represent individual districts. Instead, they represented specific classes. Because of this drastically different approach to government, the British did not understand the colonists' statement that they had no representation in the British Parliament.

Acts of British Parliament

After the French and Indian Wars, the British Parliament passed four major acts:
- The Sugar Act, 1764—this act not only required taxes to be collected on molasses brought into the colonies, but gave British officials the right to search the homes of anyone suspected of violating it.
- The Stamp Act, 1765—this act taxed printed materials such as newspapers and legal documents. Protests led the Stamp Act to be repealed in 1766, but the repeal also included the Declaratory Act, which stated that Parliament had the right to govern the colonies.
- The Quartering Act, 1765—this act required colonists to provide accommodations and supplies for British troops. In addition, colonists were prohibited from settling west of the Appalachians until given permission by Britain.
- The Townshend Acts, 1767—these acts taxed paper, paint, lead and tea that came into the colonies. Colonists led boycotts in protest, and in Massachusetts leaders like Samuel and John Adams began to organize resistance against British rule.

Boston Massacre

With the passage of the Stamp Act, nine colonies met in New York to demand its repeal. Elsewhere, protest arose in New York City, Philadelphia, Boston and other cities. These protests sometimes escalated into violence, often targeting ruling British officials. The passage of the Townshend Acts in 1767 led to additional tension in the colonies. The British sent troops to New York City and Boston. On March 5, 1770, protesters began to taunt the British troops, throwing snowballs. The soldiers responded by firing into the crowd. This clash between protesters and soldiers led to five deaths and eight injuries, and was christened the Boston Massacre. Shortly thereafter, Britain repealed the majority of the Townshend Acts.

Tea Act and the Boston Tea Party

The majority of the Townshend Acts were repealed after the Boston Massacre in 1770, but Britain kept the tax on tea. In 1773, the Tea Act was passed. This allowed the East India Company to sell tea for much lower prices, and also allowed them to bypass American

- 6 -

distributors, selling directly to shopkeepers instead. Colonial tea merchants saw this as a direct assault on their business. In December of 1773, the Sons of Liberty boarded ships in Boston Harbor and dumped 342 chests of tea into the sea in protest of the new laws. This act of protest came to be known as the Boston Tea Party.

Coercive/Intolerable Acts

The Coercive Acts passed by Britain in 1774 were meant to punish Massachusetts for defying British authority. The four acts, also known as the Intolerable Acts:
- Shut down ports in Boston until the city paid back the value of the tea destroyed during the Boston Tea Party
- Required that local government officials in Massachusetts be appointed by the governor rather than being elected by the people
- Allowed trials of British soldiers to be transferred to Britain rather than being held in Massachusetts
- Required locals to provide lodging for British soldiers any time there was a disturbance, even if lodging required them to stay in private homes

These Acts led to the assembly of the First Continental Congress in Philadelphia on September 5, 1774. Fifty-five delegates met, representing 12 of the American colonies. They sought compromise with England over England's increasingly harsh efforts to control the colonies.

First Continental Congress

The First Continental Congress met in Philadelphia on September 5, 1774. Their goal was to achieve a peaceful agreement with Britain. Made up of delegates from 12 of the 13 colonies, the Congress affirmed loyalty to Britain and the power of Parliament to dictate foreign affairs in the colonies. However, they demanded that the Intolerable Acts be repealed, and instituted a trade embargo with Britain until this came to pass.

In response, George III of England declared that the American colonies must submit or face military action. The British sought to end assemblies that opposed their policies. These assemblies gathered weapons and began to form militias. On April 19, 1775, the British military was ordered to disperse a meeting of the Massachusetts Assembly. A battle ensued on Lexington Common as the armed colonists resisted. The resulting battles became the Battle of Lexington and Concord—the first battles of the American Revolution.

Second Continental Congress

The Second Continental Congress met in Philadelphia on May 10, 1775, a month after Lexington and Concord. Their discussions centered on defense of the American colonies and how to conduct the growing war, as well as local government. The delegates also discussed declaring independence from Britain, with many members in favor of this drastic move. They established an army, and on June 15, named George Washington as its commander-in-chief. By 1776, it was obvious that there was no turning back from full-scale war with Britain. The colonial delegates of the Continental Congress drafted the Declaration of Independence on July 4, 1776.

Declaration of Independence

Penned by Thomas Jefferson and signed on July 4, 1776, the Declaration of Independence stated that King George III had violated the rights of the colonists and was establishing a tyrannical reign over them. Many of Jefferson's ideas of natural rights and property rights were shaped by seventeenth-century philosopher John Locke. Jefferson asserted all people's rights to "life, liberty and the pursuit of happiness." Locke's comparable idea asserted "life, liberty, and private property." Both felt that the purpose of government was to protect the rights of the people, and that individual rights were more important than individuals' obligations to the state.

Battles of the Revolutionary War

The following are five major battles of the Revolutionary War and their significance:
- The Battle of Lexington and Concord (April 1775) is considered the first engagement of the Revolutionary War.
- The Battle of Bunker Hill (June 1775) was one of the bloodiest of the entire war. Although American troops withdrew, about half of the British army was lost. The colonists proved they could stand against professional British soldiers. In August, Britain declared that the American colonies were officially in a state of rebellion.
- The first colonial victory occurred in Trenton, New Jersey, when Washington and his troops crossed the Delaware River on Christmas Day, 1776 for a December 26 surprise attack on British and Hessian troops.

- The Battle of Saratoga effectively ended a plan to separate the New England colonies from their Southern counterparts. The surrender of British general John Burgoyne led to France joining the war as allies of the Americans, and is generally considered a turning point of the war. *diverted resources from British*
- On October 19, 1781, General Cornwallis surrendered after a defeat in the Battle of Yorktown, ending the Revolutionary War.

Treaty of Paris

The Treaty of Paris was signed on September 3, 1783, bringing an official end to the Revolutionary War. In this document, Britain officially recognized the United States of America as an independent nation. The treaty established the Mississippi River as the country's western border. The treaty also restored Florida to Spain, while France reclaimed African and Caribbean colonies seized by the British in 1763. On November 25, 1783, the last British troops departed from the newly born United States of America.

Articles of Confederation

A precursor to the Constitution, the Articles of Confederation represented the first attempt of the newly independent colonies to establish the basics of government. The Continental Congress approved the Articles on November 15, 1777. They went into effect on March 1, 1781, following ratification by the thirteen states. The Articles prevented a central government from gaining too much power, instead giving power to a Congressional body made up of delegates from all thirteen states. However, the individual states retained final authority.

Without a strong central executive, though, this weak alliance among the new states proved ineffective in settling disputes or enforcing laws. The idea of a weak central government needed to be revised. Recognition of these weaknesses eventually led to the drafting of a new document, the Constitution.

The Constitution

Delegates from twelve of the thirteen states (Rhode Island was not represented) met in Philadelphia in May of 1787, initially intending to revise the Articles of Confederation. However, it quickly became apparent that a simple revision would not provide the workable governmental structure the newly formed country needed. After vowing to keep all the proceedings secret until the final document was completed, the delegates set out to draft what would eventually become the Constitution of the United States of America. By keeping the negotiations secret, the delegates were able to present a completed document to the country for ratification, rather than having every small detail hammered out by the general public.

Structure of proposed government

The delegates agreed that the new nation required a strong central government, but that its overall power should be limited. The various branches of the government should have balanced power, so that no one group could control the others. Final power belonged with the citizens who voted officials into office based on who would provide the best representation.

Virginia Plan, New Jersey Plan, and the Great Compromise

Disagreement immediately occurred between delegates from large states and those from smaller states. James Madison and Edmund Randolph (the governor of Virginia) felt that representation in Congress should be based on state population. This was the Virginia Plan. The New Jersey Plan, presented by William Paterson, from New Jersey, proposed each state have equal representation. Finally, Roger Sherman from Connecticut formulated the Connecticut Compromise, also called the Great Compromise. The result was the familiar structure we have today. Each state has the equal representation of two Senators in the Senate, with the number of representatives in the House of Representatives based on population. This is called a bicameral Congress. Both houses may draft bills, but financial matters must originate in the House of Representatives.

Three-fifths compromise

During debate on the US Constitution, a disagreement arose between the Northern and Southern states involving how slaves should be counted when determining a state's quota of representatives. In the South large numbers of slaves were commonly used to run plantations. Delegates wanted slaves to be counted to determine the number of representatives, but not counted to determine the amount of taxes the states would pay. The Northern states wanted exactly the opposite arrangement. The final decision was to count three-fifths of the slave population both for tax purposes and to determine representation. This was called the three-fifths compromise.

Commerce Compromise

The Commerce Compromise also resulted from a North/South disagreement. In the North the economy was centered on industry and trade. The Southern economy was largely agricultural. The Northern states wanted to give the new government the ability to regulate exports as well as trade between the states. The South opposed this plan. Another compromise was in order. In the end, Congress received regulatory power over all trade, including the ability to collect tariffs on exported goods. In the South, this raised another red flag regarding the slave trade, as they were concerned about the effect on their economy if tariffs were levied on slaves. The final agreement allowed importing slaves to continue for twenty years without government intervention. Import taxes on slaves were limited, and after the year 1808, Congress could decide whether to allow continued imports of slaves.

Objections against the Constitution

Once the Constitution was drafted, it was presented for approval by the states. Nine states needed to approve the document for it to become official. However, debate and discussion continued. Major concerns included:
- The lack of a bill of rights to protect individual freedoms
- States felt too much power was being handed over to the central government
- Voters wanted more control over their elected representatives

Discussion about necessary changes to the Constitution was divided into two camps: Federalists and Anti-Federalists. Federalists wanted a strong central government. Anti-Federalists wanted to prevent a tyrannical government from developing if a central government held too much power.

Federalist and Anti-Federalist camps

Major Federalist leaders included Alexander Hamilton, John Jay and James Madison. They wrote a series of letters, called the Federalist Papers, aimed at convincing the states to ratify the Constitution. These were published in New York papers. Anti-Federalists included Thomas Jefferson and Patrick Henry. They argued against the Constitution as it was originally drafted in a series of Anti-Federalist Papers.

The final compromise produced a strong central government controlled by checks and balances. A Bill of Rights was also added, becoming the first ten amendments to the Constitution. These amendments protected rights such as freedom of speech, freedom of religion, and other basic rights. Aside from various amendments added throughout the years, the United States Constitution has remained unchanged.

Administration of the new government

The individuals who formed the first administration of the new government were:
- George Washington—elected as the first President of the United States in 1789
- John Adams—finished second in the election and became the first Vice President
- Thomas Jefferson—appointed by Washington as Secretary of State
- Alexander Hamilton—appointed Secretary of the Treasury

Alien and Sedition Acts

When John Adams became president, a war was raging between Britain and France. While Adams and the Federalists backed the British, Thomas Jefferson and the Republican Party supported the French. The United States nearly went to war with France during this time period, while France worked to spread its international standing and influence under the leadership of Napoleon Bonaparte. The Alien and Sedition Acts grew out of this conflict, and made it illegal to speak in a hostile fashion against the existing government. They also allowed the president to deport anyone in the US who was not a citizen and who was suspected of treason or treasonous activity. When Jefferson became the third president in 1800, he repealed these four laws and pardoned anyone who had been convicted under them.

> ➤ **Review Video:** The Alien and Sedition Acts
> *Visit* ***mometrix.com/academy*** *and enter* ***Code***: **633780**

Political parties

Many in the US were against political parties after seeing the way parties, or factions, functioned in Britain. The factions in Britain were more interested in personal profit than the overall good of the country, and they did not want this to happen in the US.

However, the differences of opinion between Thomas Jefferson and Alexander Hamilton led to formation of political parties. Hamilton favored a stronger central government, while Jefferson felt that more power should remain with the states. Jefferson was in favor of strict Constitutional interpretation, while Hamilton believed in a more flexible approach. As others joined the two camps, Hamilton backers began to term themselves Federalists while those supporting Jefferson became identified as Democratic-Republicans.

Whig Party, Democratic Party, and Republican Party

Thomas Jefferson was elected president in 1800 and again in 1804. The Federalist Party began to decline, and its major figure, Alexander Hamilton, died in a duel with Aaron Burr in 1804. By 1816, the Federalist Party had virtually disappeared.

New parties sprang up to take its place. After 1824, the Democratic-Republican Party suffered a split. The Whigs rose, backing John Quincy Adams and industrial growth. The new Democratic Party formed, in opposition to the Whigs, and their candidate, Andrew Jackson, was elected as president in 1828.

By the 1850s, issues regarding slavery led to the formation of the Republican Party, which was anti-slavery, while the Democratic Party, with a larger interest in the South, favored slavery. This Republican/Democrat division formed the basis of today's two-party system.

Marbury v. Madison

The main duty of the Supreme Court today is judicial review. This power was largely established by Marbury v. Madison. When John Adams was voted out of office in 1800, he worked, during his final days in office, to appoint Federalist judges to Supreme Court positions, knowing Jefferson, his replacement, held opposing views. As late as March 3, the day before Jefferson was to take office, Adams made last-minute appointments referred to as "Midnight Judges." One of the late appointments was William Marbury. The next day, March 4, Jefferson ordered his Secretary of State, James Madison, not to deliver Marbury's commission. This decision was backed by Chief Justice Marshall, who determined that the Judiciary Act of 1789, which granted the power to deliver commissions, was illegal in that it gave the Judicial Branch powers not granted in the Constitution. This case set precedent for the Supreme Court to nullify laws it found to be unconstitutional.

> **Review Video:** Marbury v. Madison
> *Visit **mometrix.com/academy** and enter **Code**: 270990*

McCulloch v. Maryland

Judicial review was further exercised by the Supreme Court in McCulloch v. Maryland. When Congress chartered a national bank, the Second Bank of the United States, Maryland voted to tax any bank business dealing with banks chartered outside the state, including the federally chartered bank. Andrew McCulloch, an employee of the Second Bank of the US in Baltimore, refused to pay this tax. The resulting lawsuit from the State of Maryland went to the Supreme Court for judgment.

John Marshall, Chief Justice of the Supreme Court, stated that Congress was within its rights to charter a national bank. In addition, the State of Maryland did not have the power to levy a tax on the federal bank or on the federal government in general. In cases where state and federal government collided, precedent was set for the federal government to prevail.

Effects of the Treaty of Paris on Native Americans

After the Revolutionary War, the Treaty of Paris, which outlined the terms of surrender of the British to the Americans, granted large parcels of land to the US that were occupied by Native Americans. The new government attempted to claim the land, treating the natives as a conquered people. This approach proved unenforceable.

Next, the government tried purchasing the land from the Indians via a series of treaties as the country expanded westward. In practice, however, these treaties were not honored, and Native Americans were simply dislocated and forced to move farther and farther west, often with military action, as American expansion continued.

Indian Removal Act of 1830 and the Treaty of New Echota

The Indian Removal Act of 1830 gave the new American government power to form treaties with Native Americans. In theory, America would claim land east of the Mississippi in exchange for land west of the Mississippi, to which the natives would relocate voluntarily. In practice, many tribal leaders were forced into signing the treaties, and relocation at times occurred by force. The Treaty of New Echota in 1835 was supposedly a treaty between the US government and Cherokee tribes in Georgia. However, the treaty was not signed by tribal leaders, but rather by a small portion of the represented people. The leaders protested and refused to leave, but President Martin Van Buren enforced the treaty by sending soldiers. During their forced relocation, more than 4,000 Cherokee Indians died on what became known as the Trail of Tears.

1830: New Echota
Van Buran + Trail of tears

Early economic trends by region

In the Northeast, the economy mostly depended on manufacturing, industry, and industrial development. This led to a dichotomy between rich business owners and industrial leaders and the much poorer workers who supported their businesses. The South continued to depend on agriculture, especially on large-scale farms or plantations worked mostly by slaves and indentured servants. In the West, where new settlements had begun to develop, the land was largely wild. Growing communities were essentially agricultural, raising crops and livestock. The differences between regions led each to support different interests both politically and economically.

Louisiana Purchase

With tension still high between France and Britain, Napoleon was in need of money to support his continuing war efforts. To secure necessary funds, he decided to sell the Louisiana Territory to the US President Thomas Jefferson wanted to buy New Orleans, feeling US trade was made vulnerable to both Spain and France at that port. Instead, Napoleon sold him the entire territory for the bargain price of fifteen million dollars. The Louisiana Territory was larger than all the rest of the United States put together, and it eventually became fifteen additional states. Federalists in Congress were opposed to the purchase. They feared that the Louisiana Purchase would extend slavery, and that further western growth would weaken the power of the northern states.

Early foreign policy

The three major ideas driving American foreign policy during its early years were:
- Isolationism—the early US government did not intend to establish colonies, though they did plan to grow larger within the bounds of North America.
- No entangling alliances—both George Washington and Thomas Jefferson were opposed to forming any permanent alliances with other countries or becoming involved in other countries' internal issues.
- Nationalism—a positive patriotic feeling about the United States blossomed quickly among its citizens, particularly after the War of 1812, when the US once again defeated Britain. The Industrial Revolution also sparked increased nationalism by allowing even the most far-flung areas of the US to communicate with each other via telegraph and the expanding railroad.

War of 1812

The War of 1812 grew out of the continuing tension between France and Great Britain. Napoleon continued striving to conquer Britain, while the US continued trade with both countries, but favored France and the French colonies. Because of what Britain saw as an alliance between America and France, they determined to bring an end to trade between the two nations.

With the British preventing US trade with the French and the French preventing trade with the British, James Madison's presidency introduced acts to regulate international trade. If either Britain or France removed their restrictions, America would not trade with the other

- 13 -

country. Napoleon acted first, and Madison prohibited trade with England. England saw this as the US formally siding with the French, and war ensued in 1812.

The War of 1812 has been called the Second American Revolution. It established the superiority of the US naval forces and reestablished US independence from Britain and Europe.

The British had two major objections to America's continued trade with France. First, they saw the US as helping France's war effort by providing supplies and goods. Second, the United States had grown into a competitor, taking trade and money away from British ships and tradesmen. In its attempts to end American trade with France, the British put into effect the Orders in Council, which made any and all French-owned ports off-limits to American ships. They also began to seize American ships and conscript their crews.

> **Review Video:** Opinions About the War of 1812
> Visit *mometrix.com/academy* and enter *Code*: **274558**

> **Review Video:** Results of the War of 1812
> Visit *mometrix.com/academy* and enter *Code*: **993725**

Military events

Two major naval battles, at Lake Erie and Lake Champlain, kept the British from invading the US via Canada. American attempts to conquer Canadian lands were not successful.

In another memorable British attack, the British invaded Washington DC and burned the White House on August 24, 1814. Legend has it that Dolley Madison, the First Lady, salvaged the portrait of George Washington from the fire. On Christmas Eve, 1814, the Treaty of Ghent officially ended the war. However, Andrew Jackson, unaware that the war was over, managed another victory at New Orleans on January 8, 1815. This victory improved American morale and led to a new wave of national pride and support known as the "Era of Good Feelings."

Monroe Doctrine

On December 2, 1823, President Monroe delivered a message to Congress in which he introduced the Monroe Doctrine. In this address, he stated that any attempts by European powers to establish new colonies on the North American continent would be considered interference in American politics. The US would stay out of European matters, and expected Europe to offer America the same courtesy. This approach to foreign policy stated in no uncertain terms that America would not tolerate any new European colonies in the New World, and that events occurring in Europe would no longer influence the policies and doctrines of the US.

Lewis and Clark Expedition

The purchase of the Louisiana Territory from France in 1803 more than doubled the size of the United States. President Thomas Jefferson wanted to have the area mapped and explored, since much of the territory was wilderness. He chose Meriwether Lewis and William Clark to head an expedition into the Louisiana Territory. After two years, Lewis and

Clark returned, having traveled all the way to the Pacific Ocean. They brought maps, detailed journals, and a multitude of information about the wide expanse of land they had traversed. The Lewis and Clark Expedition opened up the west in the Louisiana Territory and beyond for further exploration and settlement.

> ➤ **Review Video:** The Lewis and Clark Expedition
> *Visit **mometrix.com/academy** and enter **Code: 241256***

Manifest Destiny

In the 1800s, many believed America was destined by God to expand west, bringing as much of the North American continent as possible under the umbrella of US government. With the Northwest Ordinance and the Louisiana Purchase, over half of the continent became American. However, the rapid and relentless expansion brought conflict with the Native Americans, Great Britain, Mexico and Spain. One result of "Manifest Destiny" was the Mexican-American War from 1846 to 1848. By the end of the war, Texas, California, and a large portion of what is now the American Southwest joined the growing nation. Conflict also arose over the Oregon territory, shared by the US and Britain. In 1846, President James Polk resolved this problem by compromising with Britain, establishing a US boundary south of the 49th parallel.

> ➤ **Review Video:** Manifest Destiny
> *Visit **mometrix.com/academy** and enter **Code: 962946***

Mexican-American War

Spain had held colonial interests in America since the 1540s—earlier even than Great Britain. In 1810, Mexico revolted against Spain and became a free nation in 1821. Texas followed suit, declaring its independence after an 1836 revolution. In 1844, the Democrats pressed President Tyler to annex Texas. Unlike his predecessor, Andrew Jackson, Tyler agreed to admit Texas into the Union and in 1845 Texas became a state.

During Mexico's war for independence, the nation incurred $4.5 million in war debts to the US Polk offered to forgive the debts in return for New Mexico and Upper California, but Mexico refused. In 1846, war was declared in response to a Mexican attack on American troops along the southern border of Texas. Additional conflict arose in Congress over the Wilmot Proviso, which proposed banning of slavery from any territory the US acquired from Mexico. The war ended in 1848.

Gadsden Purchase and the 1853 post-war treaty with Mexico

After the Mexican-American war, a second treaty in 1853 determined hundreds of miles of America's southwest borders. In 1854, the Gadsden Purchase was finalized, providing even more territory to aid in the building of the transcontinental railroad. This purchase added what would eventually become the southernmost regions of Arizona and New Mexico to the growing nation. The modern outline of the United States was by this time nearly complete.

American System

Spurred by the trade conflicts of the War of 1812, and supported by Henry Clay among others, the American System set up tariffs to help protect American interests from competition with overseas products. Reducing competition led to growth in employment and an overall increase in American industry. The higher tariffs also provided funds for the government to pay for various improvements. Congress passed high tariffs in 1816 and also chartered a federal bank. The Second Bank of the United States was given the job of regulating America's money supply.

Jacksonian Democracy

Jacksonian Democracy is largely seen as a shift from politics favoring the wealthy to politics favoring the common man. All free white males were given the right to vote, not just property owners, as had been the case previously. Jackson's approach favored the patronage system, Laissez-faire economics, and relocation of the Indian tribes from the Southeast portion of the country. Jackson opposed the formation of a federal bank and allowed the Second Band of the United States to collapse by vetoing a bill to renew the charter. Jackson also faced the challenge of the Nullification Crisis when South Carolina claimed that it could ignore or nullify any federal law it considered unconstitutional. Jackson sent troops to the state to enforce the protested tariff laws, and a compromise engineered by Henry Clay in 1833 settled the matter for the time being.

> **Review Video:** Andrew Jackson as President
> *Visit **mometrix.com/academy** and enter **Code**: **667792***

> **Review Video:** Major Issues Under Andrew Jackson
> *Visit **mometrix.com/academy** and enter **Code**: **739251***

Conflict between North and South

The conflict between North and South coalesced around the issue of slavery, but other elements contributed to the growing disagreement. Though most farmers in the South worked small farms with little or no slave labor, the huge plantations run by the South's rich depended on slaves or indentured servants to remain profitable. They had also become more dependent on cotton, with slave populations growing in concert with the rapid increase in cotton production. In the North, a more diverse agricultural economy and the growth of industry made slaves rarer. The abolitionist movement grew steadily, with Harriet Beecher Stowe's *Uncle Tom's Cabin* giving many an idea to rally around. A collection

of anti-slavery organizations formed, with many actively working to free slaves in the South, often bringing them to the northern states or Canada.

> **Review Video:** Conflict between the North and South
> *Visit **mometrix.com/academy** and enter **Code**: **219819***

Anti-slavery organizations

Five anti-slavery organizations and their significance are:
- American Colonization Society—Protestant churches formed this group, aimed at returning black slaves to Africa. Former slaves subsequently formed Liberia, but the colony did not do well, as the region was not well-suited for agriculture.
- American Anti-Slavery Society—William Lloyd Garrison, a Quaker, was the major force behind this group and its newspaper, *The Liberator*.
- Philadelphia Female Anti-Slavery Society—a women-only group formed by Margaretta Forten because women were not allowed to join the Anti-Slavery Society formed by her father.
- Anti-Slavery Convention of American Women—this group continued meeting even after pro-slavery factions burned down their original meeting place.
- Female Vigilant Society—an organization that raised funds to help the Underground Railroad, as well as slave refugees.

Attitudes toward education

Horace Mann, among others, felt that schools could help children become better citizens, keep them away from crime, prevent poverty, and help American society become more unified. His *Common School Journal* brought his ideas of the importance of education into the public consciousness and proposed his suggestions for an improved American education system. Increased literacy led to increased awareness of current events, Western expansion, and other major developments of the time period. Public interest and participation in the arts and literature also increased. By the end of the 19th century, all children had access to a free public elementary education.

Transportation

As America expanded its borders, it also developed new technology to travel the rapidly growing country. Roads and railroads traversed the nation, with the Transcontinental Railroad eventually allowing travel from one coast to the other. Canals and steamboats simplified water travel and made shipping easier and less expensive. The Erie Canal (1825) connected the Great Lakes with the Hudson River. Other canals connected other major waterways, further facilitating transportation and the shipment of goods.

With growing numbers of settlers moving into the West, wagon trails developed, including the Oregon Trail, California Trail and the Santa Fe Trail. The most common vehicles seen along these westbound trails were covered wagons, also known as prairie schooners.

Industrial activity and major inventions

During the eighteenth century, goods were often manufactured in houses or small shops. With increased technology allowing for the use of machines, factories began to develop. In factories a large volume of salable goods could be produced in a much shorter amount of time. Many Americans, including increasing numbers of immigrants, found jobs in these factories, which were in constant need of labor. Another major invention was the cotton gin, which significantly decreased the processing time of cotton and was a major factor in the rapid expansion of cotton production in the South.

Labor movements

In 1751, a group of bakers held a protest in which they stopped baking bread. This was technically the first American labor strike. In the 1830s and 1840s, labor movements began in earnest. Boston's masons, carpenters and stoneworkers protested the length of the workday, fighting to reduce it to ten hours. In 1844, a group of women in the textile industry also fought to reduce their workday to ten hours, forming the Lowell Female Labor Reform Association. Many other protests occurred and organizations developed through this time period with the same goal in mind.

Second Great Awakening

Led by Protestant evangelical leaders, the Second Great Awakening occurred between 1800 and 1830. Several missionary groups grew out of the movement, including the American Home Missionary Society, which formed in 1826. The ideas behind the Second Great Awakening focused on personal responsibility, both as an individual and in response to injustice and suffering. The American Bible Society and the American Tract Society provided literature, while various traveling preachers spread the word. New denominations arose, including the Latter-day Saints and Seventh-day Adventists.

Another movement associated with the Second Great Awakening was the temperance movement, focused on ending the production and use of alcohol. One major organization behind the temperance movement was the Society for the Promotion of Temperance, formed in 1826 in Boston.

Women's rights movement

[handwritten annotations: Eliz Cady Stanton   Sojourner Truth, Ernestine Rose + Lucretia Mott]

The women's rights movement began in the 1840s with leaders including Elizabeth Cady Stanton, Sojourner Truth, Ernestine Rose, and Lucretia Mott. In 1869, Elizabeth Cady Stanton and Susan B. Anthony formed the National Woman Suffrage Association, fighting for women's right to vote.

In 1848 in Seneca Falls, the first women's rights convention was held, with about three hundred attendees. The two-day Seneca Falls Convention discussed the rights of women to vote (suffrage) as well as equal treatment in careers, legal proceedings, etc. The convention produced a "Declaration of Sentiments" which outlined a plan for women to attain the rights they deserved. Frederick Douglass supported the women's rights movement, as well as the abolition movement. In fact, women's rights and abolition movements often went hand-in-hand during this time period.

Missouri Compromise

By 1819, the United States had developed a tenuous balance between slave and free states, with exactly twenty-two senators in Congress from each faction. However, Missouri was ready to join the union. As a slave state, it would tip the balance in Congress. To prevent this imbalance, the Missouri Compromise brought the northern part of Massachusetts into the union as Maine, establishing it as a free state to balance the admission of Missouri as a slave state. In addition, the remaining portion of the Louisiana Purchase was to remain free north of latitude 36°30'. Since cotton did not grow well this far north, this limitation was acceptable to congressmen representing the slave states.

However, the proposed Missouri constitution presented a problem, as it outlawed immigration of free blacks into the state. Another compromise was in order, this time proposed by Henry Clay. According to this new compromise, Missouri's would never pass a law that prevented anyone from entering the state. Through this and other work, Clay earned his title of the "Great Compromiser."

> **Review Video:** <u>Missouri Compromise</u>
> *Visit mometrix.com/academy and enter Code*: **848091**

Popular sovereignty and the Compromise of 1850

In addition to the pro-slavery and anti-slavery factions, a third group rose who felt that each individual state should decide whether to allow or permit slavery within its borders. The idea that a state could make its own choices was referred to as popular sovereignty.

When California applied to join the union in 1849, the balance of congressional power was again threatened. The Compromise of 1850 introduced a group of laws meant to bring an end to the conflict:
- California's admittance as a free state
- The outlaw of the slave trade in Washington, D.C
- An increase in efforts to capture escaped slaves
- The right of New Mexico and Utah territories to decide individually whether to allow slavery

In spite of these measures, debate raged each time a new state prepared to enter the union.

Kansas-Nebraska Act

With the creation of the Kansas and Nebraska territories in 1854, another debate began. Congress allowed popular sovereignty in these territories, but slavery opponents argued that the Missouri Compromise had already made slavery illegal in this region. In Kansas, two separate governments arose, one pro-slavery and one anti-slavery. Conflict between the two factions rose to violence, leading Kansas to gain the nickname of "Bleeding Kansas."

> **Review Video:** <u>Sectional Crisis: The Kansas-Nebraska Act</u>
> *Visit mometrix.com/academy and enter Code*: **982119**

Dred Scott decision

Abolitionist factions coalesced around the case of Dred Scott, using his case to test the country's laws regarding slavery. Scott, a slave, had been taken by his owner from Missouri, which was a slave state. He then traveled to Illinois, a free state, then on to the Minnesota Territory, also free based on the Missouri Compromise. After several years, he returned to Missouri and his owner subsequently died. Abolitionists took Scott's case to court, stating that Scott was no longer a slave but free, since he had lived in free territory. The case went to the Supreme Court.

The Supreme Court stated that, because Scott, as a slave, was not a US citizen, his time in free states did not change his status. He also did not have the right to sue. In addition, the Court determined that the Missouri Compromise was unconstitutional, stating that Congress had overstepped its bounds by outlawing slavery in the territories.

> **Review Video:** Dred Scott Act
> Visit *mometrix.com/academy* and enter *Code*: **448931**

Harper's Ferry and John Brown

John Brown, an abolitionist, had participated in several anti-slavery activities, including killing five pro-slavery men in retaliation, after the sacking of Lawrence, Kansas, an anti-slavery town. He and other abolitionists also banded together to pool their funds and build a runaway slave colony.

In 1859, Brown seized a federal arsenal in Harper's Ferry, located in what is now West Virginia. Brown intended to seize guns and ammunition and lead a slave rebellion. Robert E. Lee captured Brown and 21 followers, who were subsequently tried and hanged. While Northerners took the executions as an indication that the government supported slavery, Southerners were of the opinion that most of the North supported Brown and were, in general, anti-slavery.

1860 election

The 1860 Presidential candidates represented four different parties, each with a different opinion on slavery:
- John Breckinridge, representing the Southern Democrats, was pro-slavery but urged compromise to preserve the Union.
- Abraham Lincoln, of the Republican Party, was anti-slavery.
- Stephen Douglas, of the Northern Democrats, felt that the issue should be determined locally, on a state-by-state basis.
- John Bell, of the Constitutional Union Party, focused primarily on keeping the Union intact.

In the end, Abraham Lincoln won both the popular and electoral election. Southern states, who had sworn to secede from the Union if Lincoln was elected did so, led by South Carolina. Shortly thereafter, the Civil War began when Confederate shots were fired on Fort Sumter in Charleston.

Advantages of the North and South in the Civil War

The Northern states had significant advantages, including:
- Larger population—the North consisted of 24 states while the South had 11.
- Better transportation and finances—with railroads primarily in the North, supply chains were much more dependable, as was overseas trade.
- Raw materials—the North held the majority of America's gold, as well as iron, copper, and other minerals vital to wartime.

The South's advantages included:
- Better-trained military officers—many of the Southern officers were West Point trained and had commanded in the Mexican and Indian wars.
- Familiarity with weapons—the climate and lifestyle of the South meant most of the people were experienced with both guns and horses. The industrial North had less extensive experience.
- Defensive position—the South felt that victory was guaranteed, since they were protecting their own lands, while the North would be invading.
- Well-defined goals—the South fought an ideological war to be allowed to govern themselves and preserve their way of life. The North originally fought to preserve the Union and later to free the slaves.

Emancipation Proclamation

The Emancipation Proclamation, issued by President Lincoln on January 1, 1863, freed all slaves in Confederate states that were still in rebellion against the Union. While the original proclamation did not free any slaves in the states actually under Union control, it did set a precedent for the emancipation of slaves as the war progressed.

The Emancipation Proclamation worked in the Union's favor as many freed slaves and other black troops joined the Union Army. Almost 200,000 blacks fought in the Union army, and over 10,000 served in the navy. By the end of the war, over 4 million slaves had been freed, and in 1865 slavery was abolished in the 13th amendment to the Constitution.

> **Review Video:** Emancipation Proclamation
> *Visit mometrix.com/academy and enter Code: 511675*

Civil War events

Six major events of the Civil War and their outcomes or significance are:
- The First Battle of Bull Run (July 21, 1861)—this was the first major land battle of the war. Observers, expecting to enjoy an entertaining skirmish, set up picnics nearby. Instead, they found themselves witness to a bloodbath. Union forces were defeated, and the battle set the course of the Civil War as long, bloody and costly.
- The Capture of Fort Henry by Ulysses S. Grant—this battle in February of 1862 marked the Union's first major victory.
- The Battle of Gettysburg (July 1-3, 1863)—often seen as the turning point of the war, Gettysburg also saw the largest number of casualties of the war, with over 50,000 dead, wounded, or missing. Robert E. Lee was defeated, and the Confederate army, significantly crippled, withdrew.
- The Overland Campaign (May and June of 1864)—Grant, now in command of all the Union armies, led this high casualty campaign that eventually positioned the Union for victory.
- Sherman's March to the Sea—William Tecumseh Sherman, in May of 1864, conquered Atlanta. He then continued to Savannah, destroying vast amounts of property as he went.
- Following Lee's defeat at the Appomattox Courthouse, General Grant accepted Lee's surrender in the home of Wilmer McLean in Appomattox, Virginia on April 9, 1865.

Lincoln's assassination

The Civil War ended with the surrender of the South on April 9, 1865. Five days later, Lincoln and his wife, Mary, attended the play *Our American Cousin* at the Ford Theater. John Wilkes Booth performed his part in a conspiracy to aid the Confederacy by shooting Lincoln in the back of the head. Booth was tracked down and killed by Union soldiers 12 days later. Lincoln, carried from the theater to a nearby house, died the next morning.

Reconstruction and the Freedmen's Bureau

In the aftermath of the Civil War, the South was left in chaos. From 1865 to 1877, government on all levels worked to help restore order to the South, ensure civil rights to the freed slaves, and bring the Confederate states back into the Union. This became known as the Reconstruction period. In 1866, Congress passed the Reconstruction Acts, placing former Confederate states under military rule and stating the grounds for readmission into the Union.

The Freedmen's Bureau was formed to help freedmen both with basic necessities like food and clothing and also with employment and finding of family members who had been separated during the war. Many in the South felt the Freedmen's Bureau worked to set freed slaves against their former owners. The Bureau was intended to help former slaves become self-sufficient, and to keep them from falling prey to those who would take advantage of them. It eventually closed due to lack of funding and to violence from the Ku Klux Klan.

Radical and Moderate Republicans

The Radical Republicans wished to treat the South quite harshly after the war. Thaddeus Stevens, the House Leader, suggested that the Confederate states be treated as if they were territories again, with ten years of military rule and territorial government before they would be readmitted. He also wanted to give all black men the right to vote. Former Confederate soldiers would be required to swear they had never supported the Confederacy (knows as the "Ironclad Oath") in order to be granted full rights as American citizens.

In contrast, the moderate Republicans wanted only black men who were literate or who had served as Union troops to be able to vote. All Confederate soldiers except troop leaders would also be able to vote. Before his death, Lincoln had favored a more moderate approach to Reconstruction, hoping this approach might bring some states back into the Union before the end of the war.

Black Codes, the Civil Rights Act, and impeachment of Andrew Johnson

The Black Codes were proposed to control freed slaves. They would not be allowed to bear arms, assemble, serve on juries, or testify against whites. Schools would be segregated, and unemployed blacks could be arrested and forced to work. The Civil Rights Act countered these codes, providing much wider rights for the freed slaves. Andrew Johnson, who became president after Lincoln's death, supported the Black Codes and vetoed the Civil Rights Act in 1865 and again in 1866. The second time, Congress overrode his veto and it became law. Two years later, Congress voted to impeach Johnson, the culmination of tensions between Congress and the president. He was tried and came within a single vote of being convicted, but ultimately was acquitted and finished his term in office.

Thirteenth, Fourteenth and Fifteenth Amendments

The Thirteenth, Fourteenth and Fifteenth Amendments were all passed shortly after the end of the Civil War:
- The Thirteenth Amendment was ratified by the states on December 6, 1865. This amendment prohibited slavery in the United States.
- The Fourteenth Amendment overturned the Dred Scott decision, and was ratified July 9, 1868. American citizenship was redefined: a citizen was any person born or naturalized in the US, with all citizens guaranteed equal protection by all states. It also guaranteed citizens of any race the right to file a lawsuit or serve on a jury.
- The Fifteenth Amendment was ratified February 3, 1870. It states that no citizen of the United States can be denied the right to vote based on race, color, or previous status as a slave.

> ➤ **Review Video:** The 13th Amendment
> *Visit mometrix.com/academy and enter Code:* **867407**

> ➤ **Review Video:** The 14th Amendment
> *Visit mometrix.com/academy and enter Code:* **928755**

> ➤ **Review Video:** The 15th Amendment
> *Visit mometrix.com/academy and enter Code:* **102009**

Reconstruction

The three phases of Reconstruction are:
- Presidential Reconstruction—largely driven by President Andrew Johnson's policies, the Presidential phase of Reconstruction was lenient on the South and allowed continued discrimination against and control over blacks.
- Congressional Reconstruction—Congress, controlled largely by Radical Republicans, took a different stance, providing a wider range of civil rights for blacks and greater control over Southern government. Congressional Reconstruction is marked by military control of the former Confederate States.
- Redemption—gradually, the Confederate states were readmitted into the union. During this time, white Democrats took over the government of most of the South. In 1877, President Rutherford Hayes withdrew the last federal troops from the South.

Carpetbaggers and Scalawags

The chaos in the south attracted a number of people seeking to fill the power vacuums and take advantage of the economic disruption. Scalawags were southern Whites who aligned with Freedmen to take over local governments. Many in the South who could have filled political offices refused to take the necessary oath required to grant them the right to vote, leaving many opportunities for Scalawags and others. Carpetbaggers were northerners who traveled to the South for various reasons. Some provided assistance, while others sought to make money or to acquire political power during this chaotic period.

Transcontinental railroad

In 1869, the Union Pacific Railroad completed the first section of a planned transcontinental railroad. This section went from Omaha, Nebraska to Sacramento, California. Ninety percent of the workers were Chinese, working in very dangerous conditions for very low pay. With the rise of the railroad, products were much more easily transported across the country. While this was positive overall for industry throughout the country, it was often damaging to family farmers, who found themselves paying high shipping costs for smaller supply orders while larger companies received major discounts.

Immigration limits

In 1870, the Naturalization Act put limits on US citizenship, allowing full citizenship only to whites and those of African descent. The Chinese Exclusion Act of 1882 put limits on Chinese immigration. The Immigration Act of 1882 taxed immigrants, charging fifty cents per person. These funds helped pay administrative costs for regulating immigration. Ellis Island opened in 1892 as a processing center for those arriving in New York. 1921 saw the Emergency Quota Act passed, also known as the Johnson Quota Act, which severely limited the number of immigrants allowed into the country.

Nineteenth century changes in agriculture

Technological advancements
During the mid 1800s, irrigation techniques improved significantly. Advances occurred in cultivation and breeding, as well as fertilizer use and crop rotation. In the Great Plains, also known as the Great American Desert, the dense soil was finally cultivated with steel plows. In 1892, gasoline-powered tractors arrived, and were widely used by 1900. Other advancements in agriculture's toolset included barbed wire fences, combines, silos, deep-water wells, and the cream separator.

Government actions
Four major government actions that helped improve US agriculture in the nineteenth century are:
- The Department of Agriculture came into being in 1862, working for the interests of farmers and ranchers across the country.
- The Morrill Land-Grant Acts were a series of acts passed between 1862 and 1890, allowing land-grant colleges.
- In conjunction with land-grant colleges, the Hatch Act of 1887 brought agriculture experiment stations into the picture, helping discover new farming techniques.
- In 1914, the Smith-Lever Act provided cooperative programs to help educate people about food, home economics, community development and agriculture. Related agriculture extension programs helped farmers increase crop production to feed the rapidly growing nation.

Inventors and inventions

Major inventors from the 1800s and their inventions are:
- Alexander Graham Bell—the telephone
- Orville and Wilbur Wright—the airplane
- Richard Gatling—the machine gun
- Walter Hunt, Elias Howe and Isaac Singer—the sewing machine
- Nikola Tesla—alternating current
- George Eastman—the Kodak camera
- Thomas Edison—light bulbs, motion pictures, the phonograph
- Samuel Morse—the telegraph
- Charles Goodyear—vulcanized rubber
- Cyrus McCormick—the reaper
- George Westinghouse—the transformer, the air brake

This was an active period for invention, with about 700,000 patents registered between 1860 and 1900.

Gilded Age

The time period from the end of the Civil War to the beginning of the First World War is often referred to as the Gilded Age, or the Second Industrial Revolution. The US was changing from an agricultural-based economy to an industrial economy, with rapid growth accompanying the shift. In addition, the country itself was expanding, spreading into the seemingly unlimited West.

This time period saw the beginning of banks, department stores, chain stores, and trusts—all familiar features of the modern-day landscape. Cities also grew rapidly, and large numbers of immigrants arrived in the country, swelling the urban ranks.

> ➤ **Review Video:** The Gilded Age: An Overview
> *Visit **mometrix.com/academy** and enter **Code**:* **684770**

Populist Party

A major recession struck the United States during the 1890s, with crop prices falling dramatically. Drought compounded the problems, leaving many American farmers in crippling debt. The Farmers' Alliance formed in 1875, drawing the rural poor into a single political entity.

Recession also affected the more industrial parts of the country. The Knights of Labor, formed in 1869 by Uriah Stephens, was able to unite workers into a union to protect their rights. Dissatisfied by views espoused by industrialists, these two groups, the Farmers Alliance and the Knights of Labor, joined to form the Populist Party, also known as the People's Party, in 1892. Some of the elements of the party's platform included:
- National currency
- Graduated income tax
- Government ownership of railroads as well as telegraph and telephone systems

- Secret ballots for voting
- Immigration restriction
- Single-term limits for President and Vice-President

The Populist Party was in favor of decreasing elitism and making the voice of the common man more easily heard in the political process.

Labor movement

One of the first large, well-organized strikes occurred in 1892. Called the Homestead Strike, it occurred when the Amalgamated Association of Iron and Steel Workers struck against the Carnegie Steel Company. Gunfire ensued, and Carnegie was able to eliminate the plant's union. In 1894, workers in the American Railway Union, led by Eugene Debs, initiated the Pullman Strike after the Pullman Palace Car Co. cut their wages by 28 percent. President Grover Cleveland called in troops to break up the strike on the grounds that it interfered with mail delivery. Mary Harris "Mother" Jones organized the Children's Crusade to protest child labor. A protest march proceeded to the home of President Theodore Roosevelt in 1903. Jones also worked with the United Mine Workers of America, and helped found the Industrial Workers of the World.

> ➤ **Review Video:** The Gilded Age: Labor Strikes
> *Visit **mometrix.com/academy** and enter **Code**: **683116**

> ➤ **Review Video:** The Gilded Age: Labor Unions
> *Visit **mometrix.com/academy** and enter **Code**: **749692**

Panic of 1893

Far from a US-centric event, the Panic of 1893 was an economic crisis that affected most of the globe. As a response, President Grover Cleveland repealed the Sherman Silver Purchase Act, afraid it had caused the downturn rather than boosting the economy as intended. The Panic led to bankruptcies, with banks and railroads going under and factory unemployment rising as high as 25 percent. In the end, the Republican Party regained power due to the economic crisis.

Progressive Era

From the 1890s to the end of the First World War, Progressives set forth an ideology that drove many levels of society and politics. The Progressives were in favor of workers' rights and safety, and wanted measures taken against waste and corruption. They felt science could help improve society, and that the government could—and should—provide answers to a variety of social problems. Progressives came from a wide variety of backgrounds, but were united in their desire to improve society.

Muckrakers

"Muckrakers" was a term used to identify aggressive investigative journalists who exposed scandals, corruption, and many other wrongs in late nineteenth century society. Among these intrepid writers were:

- Ida Tarbell—she exposed John D. Rockefeller's Standard Oil Trust.
- Jacob Riis—a photographer, he brought the living conditions of the poor in New York to the public's attention.
- Lincoln Steffens—he worked to expose political corruption in municipal government.
- Upton Sinclair—his book *The Jungle* led to reforms in the meat-packing industry.

Through the work of these journalists, many new policies came into being, including workmen's compensation, child labor laws, and trust-busting.

Sixteenth, Seventeenth, Eighteenth and Nineteenth Amendments

The early twentieth century saw several amendments made to the US Constitution:

- The Sixteenth Amendment (1913) established a federal income tax.
- The Seventeenth Amendment (1913) allowed popular election of senators.
- The Eighteenth Amendment (1919) prohibited the sale, production and transportation of alcohol. This amendment was later repealed by the Twenty-first Amendment.
- The Nineteenth Amendment (1920) gave women the right to vote.

These amendments largely grew out of the Progressive Era, as many citizens worked to improve American society.

Federal Trade Commission and elimination of trusts

Muckrakers such as Ida Tarbell and Lincoln Steffens brought to light the damaging trend of trusts—huge corporations working to monopolize areas of commerce so they could control prices and distribution. The Sherman Antitrust Act and the Clayton Antitrust Act set out guidelines for competition among corporations and set out to eliminate these trusts. The Federal Trade Commission was formed in 1914 in order to enforce antitrust measures and ensure that companies were operated fairly and did not create controlling monopolies.

> **Review Video:** The Progressive Era
> *Visit **mometrix.com/academy** and enter **Code**: 293582*

Government dealings with Native Americans

America's westward expansion led to conflict and violent confrontations with Native Americans such as the Battle of Little Bighorn. In 1876, the American government ordered all Indians to relocate to reservations. Lack of compliance led to the Dawes Act in 1887, which ordered assimilation rather than separation: Native Americans were offered American citizenship and a piece of their tribal land if they would accept the lot chosen by the government and live on it separately from the tribe. This act remained in effect until 1934. Reformers also forced Indian children to attend Indian Boarding Schools, where they were not allowed to speak their native language and were immersed into a Euro-American culture and religion. Children were often abused in these schools, and were indoctrinated to abandon their identity as Native Americans. In 1890, the massacre at Wounded Knee, accompanied by Geronimo's surrender, led the Native Americans to work to preserve their culture rather than fight for their lands.

Native Americans in wartime
The Spanish-American war (1898) saw a number of Native Americans serving with Teddy Roosevelt in the Rough Riders. Apache scouts accompanied General John J. Pershing to Mexico, hoping to find Pancho Villa. More than 17,000 Native Americans were drafted into service for World War I, though at the time they were not considered legal citizens. In 1924, Indians were finally granted official citizenship by the Indian Citizenship Act.

After decades of relocation, forced assimilation, and genocide, the number of Native Americans in the US has greatly declined. Though many Native Americans have chosen—or have been forced—to assimilate, about 300 reservations exist today, with most of their inhabitants living in abject poverty.

Spanish-American War

Spain had controlled Cuba since the fifteenth century. Over the centuries, the Spanish had quashed a variety of revolts. In 1886, slavery ended in Cuba, and another revolt was rising. In the meantime, the US had expressed interest in Cuba, offering Spain $130 million for the island in 1853, during Franklin Pierce's presidency. In 1898, the Cuban revolt was underway. In spite of various factions supporting the Cubans, the US President, William McKinley, refused to recognize the rebellion, preferring negotiation over involvement in war. Then the *Maine*, a US battleship in Havana Harbor, was blown up, killing 266 crew members. The US declared war two months later, and the war ended with a Spanish surrender in less than four months.

Panama Canal

Initial work began on the Panama Canal in 1881, though the idea had been discussed since the 1500s. The canal greatly reduces the length and time needed to sail from one ocean to the other by connecting the Atlantic to the Pacific through the Isthmus of Panama, which joins South America to North America. Before the canal was built, travelers had to sail around the entire perimeter of South America to reach the West Coast of the US. The French began the work after successfully completing the Suez Canal, which connected the Mediterranean Sea to the Red Sea. However, due to disease and high expense the work moved slowly and after eight years the company went bankrupt, suspending work. The US purchased the holdings, and the first ship sailed through the canal in 1914. The Panama Canal was constructed as a lock-and-lake canal, with ships lifted on locks to travel from one lake to another over the rugged, mountainous terrain. In order to maintain control of the Canal Zone, the US assisted Panama in its battle for independence from Columbia.

Roosevelt's "Big Stick Diplomacy" and foreign policy in South America

Theodore Roosevelt's famous quote, "Speak softly and carry a big stick," is supposedly of African origins, at least according to Roosevelt. He used this proverb to justify expanded involvement in foreign affairs during his tenure as President. The US military was deployed to protect American interests in Latin America. Roosevelt also worked to maintain an equal or greater influence in Latin America than those held by European interests. As a result, the US Navy grew larger, and the US generally became more involved in foreign affairs.

Roosevelt felt that if any country was left vulnerable to control by Europe, due to economic issues or political instability, the US had not only a right to intervene, but was obligated to do so. This led to US involvement in Cuba, Nicaragua, Haiti and the Dominican Republic over several decades leading into the First and Second World Wars.

William Howard Taft's "Dollar Diplomacy"

During William Howard Taft's presidency, Taft instituted "Dollar Diplomacy." This approach was America's effort to influence Latin America and East Asia through economic rather than military means. Taft saw past efforts in these areas to be political and warlike, while his efforts focused on peaceful economic goals. His justification of the policy was to protect the Panama Canal, which was vital to US trade interests.

In spite of Taft's assurance that Dollar Diplomacy was a peaceful approach, many interventions proved violent. During Latin American revolts, such as those in Nicaragua, the US sent troops to settle the revolutions. Afterwards, bankers moved in to help support the new leaders through loans. Dollar Diplomacy continued until 1913, when Woodrow Wilson was elected President.

Woodrow Wilson's "Moral Diplomacy"

Turning away from Taft's "Dollar Diplomacy," Wilson instituted a foreign policy he referred to as "moral diplomacy." This approach still influences American foreign policy today. Wilson felt that representative government and democracy in all countries would lead to worldwide stability. Democratic governments, he felt, would be less likely to threaten American interests. He also saw the US and Great Britain as the great role models in this area, as well as champions of world peace and self-government. Free trade and international commerce would allow the US to speak out regarding world events.

Main elements of Wilson's policies included:
- Maintaining a strong military
- Promoting democracy throughout the world
- Expanding international trade to boost the American economy

First World War

World War I occurred from 1914 to 1918 and was fought largely in Europe. Triggered by the assassination of Austrian Archduke Franz Ferdinand, the war rapidly escalated. At the beginning of the conflict, Woodrow Wilson declared the US neutral. Major events influencing US involvement included:
- Sinking of the *Lusitania*—the British passenger liner RMS *Lusitania* was sunk by a German U-boat in 1915. Among the 1,000 civilian victims were over 100 American citizens. Outraged by this act, many Americans began to push for US involvement in the war, using the *Lusitania* as a rallying cry.
- German U-boat aggression—Wilson continued to keep the US out of the war, using as his 1916 reelection slogan, "He kept us out of war." While he continued to work toward an end of the war, German U-boats began to indiscriminately attack American and Canadian merchant ships carrying supplies to Germany's enemies in Europe.

- Zimmerman Telegram —the final event that brought the US into World War I was the interception of the Zimmerman Telegram (also known as the Zimmerman Note). In this telegram, Germany proposed forming an alliance with the Mexico if the US entered the war.

> **Review Video:** World War I: An Overview
> *Visit mometrix.com/academy and enter Code:* **994468**

US efforts during World War I

American railroads came under government control in December 1917. The widespread system was consolidated into a single system, with each region assigned a director. This greatly increased the efficiency of the railroad system, allowing the railroads to supply both domestic and military needs. Control returned to private ownership in 1920. In 1918, telegraph, telephone and cable services also came under Federal control, to be returned to private management the next year. The American Red Cross supported the war effort by knitting clothes for Army and Navy troops. They also helped supply hospital and refugee clothing and surgical dressings. Over eight million people participated in this effort. To generate wartime funds, the US government sold Liberty Bonds. In four issues, they sold nearly $25 billion—more than one fifth of Americans purchased them. After the war, a fifth bond drive was held, but sold "Victory Liberty Bonds."

Wilson's Fourteen Points

President Woodrow Wilson proposed Fourteen Points as the basis for a peace settlement to end the war. Presented to the US Congress in January 1918, the Fourteen Points included:
- Five points outlining general ideals
- Eight points to resolve immediate problems of political and territorial nature
- One point proposing an organization of nations (the League of Nations) with the intent of maintaining world peace

In November of that same year, Germany agreed to an armistice, assuming the final treaty would be based on the Fourteen Points. However, during the peace conference in Paris 1919, there was much disagreement, leading to a final agreement that punished Germany and the other Central Powers much more than originally intended. Henry Cabot Lodge, who had become the Foreign Relations Committee chairman in 1918, wanted an unconditional surrender from Germany and was concerned about the article in the Treaty of Versailles that gave the League of Nations power to declare war without a vote from the US Congress. A League of Nations was included in the Treaty of Versailles at Wilson's insistence. The Senate rejected the Treaty of Versailles, and in the end Wilson refused to concede to Lodge's demands. As a result, the US did not join the League of Nations.

> **Review Video:** Woodrow Wilson's Fourteen Points
> *Visit mometrix.com/academy and enter Code:* **335789**

America during the 1920s

The post-war 1920s saw many Americans moving from the farm to the city, with growing prosperity in the US. The Roaring Twenties, or the Jazz Age, was driven largely by growth in the automobile and entertainment industries. Individuals like Charles Lindbergh, the first aviator to make a solo flight cross the Atlantic Ocean, added to the American admiration of individual accomplishment. Telephone lines, distribution of electricity, highways, the radio, and other inventions brought great changes to everyday life.

<u>African-American cultural movements</u>
The Harlem Renaissance saw a number of African-American artists settling in Harlem in New York. This community produced a number of well-known artists and writers, including Langston Hughes, Nella Larsen, Zora Neale Hurston, Claude McKay, Countee Cullen and Jean Toomer. The growth of jazz, also largely driven by African Americans, defined the Jazz Age. Its unconventional, improvisational style matched the growing sense of optimism and exploration of the decade. Originating as an offshoot of the blues, jazz began in New Orleans. Some significant jazz musicians were Duke Ellington, Louis Armstrong and Jelly Roll Morton. Big Band and Swing Jazz also developed in the 1920s. Well-known musicians of this movement included Bing Crosby, Frank Sinatra, Count Basie, Benny Goodman, Billie Holiday, Ella Fitzgerald and The Dorsey Brothers.

National Origins Act of 1924

The National Origins Act (Johnson-Reed Act) placed limitations on immigration. The number of immigrants allowed into the US was based on the population of each nationality of immigrants who were living in the country in 1890. Only two percent of each nationality's 1890 population numbers were allowed to immigrate. This led to great disparities between immigrants from various nations, and Asian immigration was not allowed at all. Some of the impetus behind the Johnson-Reed Act came as a result of paranoia following the Russian Revolution. Fear of communist influences in the US led to a general fear of immigrants.

Red Scare

World War I created many jobs, but after the war ended these jobs disappeared, leaving many unemployed. In the wake of these employment changes the International Workers of the World and the Socialist Party, headed by Eugene Debs, became more and more visible. Workers initiated strikes in an attempt to regain the favorable working conditions that had been put into place before the war. Unfortunately, many of these strikes became violent, and the actions were blamed on "Reds," or Communists, for trying to spread their views into America. With the recent Bolshevik Revolution in Russia, many Americans feared a similar revolution might occur in the US. The Red Scare ensued, with many individuals jailed for supposedly holding communist, anarchist or socialist beliefs.

Growth of civil rights for African-Americans

Marcus Garvey founded the Universal Negro Improvement Association and African Communities League (UNIA-ACL), which became a large and active organization focused on building black nationalism. In 1909, the National Association for the Advancement of Colored People (NAACP) came into being, working to defeat Jim Crow laws. The NAACP also helped prevent racial segregation from becoming federal law, fought against lynchings, helped black soldiers in WWI become officers, and helped defend the Scottsboro Boys, who were unjustly accused of rape.

Ku Klux Klan

In 1866, Confederate Army veterans came together to fight against Reconstruction in the South, forming a group called the Ku Klux Klan (KKK). With white supremacist beliefs, including anti-Semitism, nativism, anti-Catholicism, and overt racism, this organization relied heavily on violence to get its message across. In 1915, they grew again in power, using a film called *The Birth of a Nation*, by D.W. Griffith, to spread their ideas. In the 1920s, the reach of the KKK spread far into the North and Midwest, and members controlled a number of state governments. Its membership and power began to decline during the Great Depression, but experienced a resurgence later.

American Civil Liberties Union

The American Civil Liberties Union (ACLU), founded in 1920, grew from the American Union Against Militarism. The ACLU helped conscientious objectors avoid going to war during WWI, and also helped those being prosecuted under the Espionage Act (1917) and the Sedition Act (1918), many of whom were immigrants. Their major goals were to protect immigrants and other citizens who were threatened with prosecution for their political beliefs, and to support labor unions, which were also under threat by the government during the Red Scare.

Anti-Defamation League

In 1913, the Anti-Defamation League was formed to prevent anti-Semitic behavior and practices. Its actions also worked to prevent all forms of racism, and to prevent individuals from being discriminated against for any reason involving their race. They spoke against the Ku Klux Klan, as well as other racist or anti-Semitic organizations. This organization still works to fight discrimination against all minorities.

Great Depression

The Great Depression, which began in 1929 with the stock market crash, grew out of several factors that had developed over the previous years including:
- Growing economic disparity between the rich and middle classes, with the rich amassing wealth much more quickly than the lower classes
- Disparity in economic distribution in industries
- Growing use of credit, leading to an inflated demand for some goods
- Government support of new industries rather than agriculture
- Risky stock market investments, leading to the stock market crash

Additional factors contributing to the Depression also included the Labor Day Hurricane in the Florida Keys (1935) and the Great Hurricane of 1938 in New England, along with the Dust Bowl in the Great Plains, which destroyed crops and resulted in the displacement of as many as 2.5 million people.

> ➤ **Review Video:** The Great Depression
> *Visit mometrix.com/academy and enter Code: 331401*

Roosevelt administration

Roosevelt's "New Deal"
Franklin D. Roosevelt was elected president in 1932 with his promise of a "New Deal" for Americans. His goals were to provide government work programs to provide jobs, wages and relief to numerous workers throughout the beleaguered US. Congress gave Roosevelt almost free rein to produce relief legislation. The goals of this legislation were:
- Relief—creating jobs for the high numbers of unemployed
- Recovery—stimulating the economy through the National Recovery Administration
- Reform—passing legislation to prevent future, similar economic crashes

The Roosevelt Administration also passed legislation regarding ecological issues, including the Soil Conservation Service, aimed at preventing another Dust Bowl.

Roosevelt's "alphabet organizations"
So-called "alphabet organizations" set up during Roosevelt's administration included:
- Civilian Conservation Corps (CCC)—provided jobs in the forestry service
- Agricultural Adjustment Administration (AAA)—increased agricultural income by adjusting both production and prices
- Tennessee Valley Authority (TVA)—organized projects to build dams in the Tennessee River for flood control and production of electricity, resulting in increased productivity for industries in the area, and easier navigation of the Tennessee River
- Public Works Administration (PWA) and Civil Works Administration (CWA)—provided a multitude of jobs, initiating over 34,000 projects
- Works Progress Administration (WPA)—helped unemployed persons to secure employment on government work projects or elsewhere

Actions taken to prevent future crashes and stabilize the economy
The Roosevelt administration passed several laws and established several institutions to initiate the "reform" portion of the New Deal, including:
- Glass-Steagall Act—separated investment from commercial banking
- Securities Exchange Commission (SEC)—helped regulate Wall Street investment practices, making them less dangerous to the overall economy
- Wagner Act—provided worker and union rights to improve relations between employees and employers
- Social Security Act of 1935—provided pensions as well as unemployment insurance

Other actions focused on insuring bank deposits and adjusting the value of American currency. Most of these regulatory agencies and government policies and programs still exist today.

Labor regulations

Three major regulations regarding labor that were passed after the Great Depression are:
- The Wagner Act (1935)—also known as the National Labor Relations Act, it established that unions were legal, protected members of unions, and required collective bargaining. This act was later amended by the Taft-Hartley Act of 1947 and the Landrum-Griffin Act of 1959, which further clarified certain elements.

- Davis-Bacon Act (1931)—provided fair compensation for contractors and subcontractors
- Walsh-Healey Act (1936)—established a minimum wage, child labor laws, safety standards, and overtime pay

World War II

<u>Interventionist and Isolationist approaches to involvement</u>
When war broke out in Europe in 1939, President Roosevelt stated that the US would remain neutral. However, his overall approach was considered "interventionist," as he was willing to provide aid to the Allies without actually entering the conflict. Thus the US supplied a wide variety of war materials to the Allied nations in the early years of the war.

Isolationists believed the US should not provide any aid to the Allies, including supplies. They felt Roosevelt, by assisting the Allies, was leading the US into a war for which it was not prepared. Led by Charles Lindbergh, the Isolationists believed that any involvement in the European conflict endangered the US by weakening its national defense.

> **Review Video:** <u>World War II: An Overview</u>
> *Visit **mometrix.com/academy** and enter **Code**: **254317***

<u>US entry into the war</u>
In 1937, Japan invaded China, prompting the US to eventually halt exports to Japan. Roosevelt also did not allow Japanese interests to withdraw money held in US banks. In 1941, General Tojo rose to power as the Japanese prime minister. Recognizing America's ability to bring a halt to Japan's expansion, he authorized the bombing of Pearl Harbor on December 7. The US responded by declaring war on Japan. Partially because of the Tripartite Pact among the Axis Powers, Germany and Italy then declared war on the US, later followed by Bulgaria, Hungary, and other Axis nations.

<u>Surrender of Germany</u>
In 1941, Hitler violated the non-aggression pact he had signed with Stalin two years earlier by invading the USSR. Stalin then joined the Allies. Stalin, Roosevelt and Winston Churchill planned to defeat Germany first, then Japan, bringing the war to an end.

In 1942-1943, the Allies drove Axis forces out of Africa. In addition, the Germans were soundly defeated at Stalingrad.

The Italian Campaign involved Allied operations in Italy between July 1943 and May 1945, including Italy's liberation. On June 6, 1944, known as D-Day, the Allies invaded France at Normandy. Soviet troops moved on the eastern front at the same time, driving German forces back. By April 25, 1945, Berlin was surrounded by Soviet troops. On May 7, Germany surrendered.

> **Review Video:** <u>World War II: Germany</u>
> *Visit **mometrix.com/academy** and enter **Code**: **951452***

Surrender of Japan

War continued with Japan after Germany's surrender. Japanese forces had taken a large portion of Southeast Asia and the Western Pacific, all the way to the Aleutian Islands in Alaska. General Doolittle bombed several Japanese cities while American troops scored a victory at Midway. Additional fighting in the Battle of the Coral Sea further weakened Japan's position. As a final blow, the US dropped two atomic bombs on Japan, one on Hiroshima and the other on Nagasaki. This was the first time atomic bombs had been used in warfare, and the devastation was horrific and demoralizing. Japan surrendered on September 2, 1945, which became V-J Day in the US.

> ➤ **Review Video:** World War II: Japan
> *Visit mometrix.com/academy and enter Code*: **313104**

442nd Regimental Combat Team, the Tuskegee Airmen, and the Navajo Code Talkers

The 442nd Regimental Combat Team consisted of Japanese-Americans fighting in Europe for the US. The most highly decorated unit per member in US history, they suffered a 93% casualty rate during the war. The Tuskegee Airmen were African-American aviators, the first black Americans allowed to fly for the military. In spite of being ineligible to become official navy pilots, they flew over 15,000 missions and were highly decorated. The Navajo Code Talkers were native Navajo who used their traditional language to transmit information among Allied forces. Because Navajo is a language and not simply a code, the Axis powers were never able to translate it. Use of Navajo Code Talkers to transmit information was instrumental in the taking of Iwo Jima and other major victories of the war.

Women during World War II

Women served widely in the military during WWII, working in numerous positions, including the Flight Nurses Corps. Women also moved into the workforce while men were overseas, leading to over 19 million women in the US workforce by 1944. Rosie the Riveter stood as a symbol of these women and a means of recruiting others to take needed positions. Women, as well as their families left behind during wartime, also grew Victory Gardens to help provide food.

Atomic bomb

The atomic bomb, developed during WWII, was the most powerful bomb ever invented. A single bomb, carried by a single plane, held enough power to destroy an entire city. This devastating effect was demonstrated with the bombing of Hiroshima and Nagasaki in 1945 in what later became a controversial move, but ended the war. The bombings resulted in as many as 150,000 immediate deaths and many more as time passed after the bombings, mostly due to radiation poisoning.

Whatever the arguments against the use of "The Bomb," the post WWII era saw many countries develop similar weapons to match the newly expanded military power of the US. The impact of those developments and use of nuclear weapons continues to haunt international relations today.

Yalta Conference and the Potsdam Conference

In February 1945, Joseph Stalin, Franklin D. Roosevelt and Winston Churchill met in Yalta to discuss the post-war treatment of the Axis nations, particularly Germany. Though Germany had not yet surrendered, its defeat was imminent. After Germany's official surrender, Joseph Stalin, Harry Truman (Roosevelt's successor), and Clement Attlee (replacing Churchill partway through the conference) met to formalize those plans.

This meeting was called the Potsdam Conference. Basic provisions of these agreements included:
- Dividing Germany and Berlin into four zones of occupation
- Demilitarization of Germany
- Poland remaining under Soviet control
- Outlawing the Nazi Party
- Trials for Nazi leaders
- Relocation of numerous German citizens
- The USSR joining the United Nations, established in 1945
- Establishment of the United Nations Security Council, consisting of the US, the UK, the USSR, China and France

Agreements made with post-war Japan

General Douglas MacArthur led the American military occupation of Japan after the country surrendered. The goals of the US occupation included removing Japan's military and making the country a democracy. A 1947 constitution removed power from the emperor and gave it to the people, as well as granting voting rights to women. Japan was no longer allowed to declare war, and a group of 28 government officials were tried for war crimes. In 1951, the US finally signed a peace treaty with Japan. This treaty allowed Japan to rearm itself for purposes of self-defense, but stripped the country of the empire it had built overseas.

Alien Registration Act and treatment of Japanese immigrants

In 1940, the US passed the Alien Registration Act, which required all aliens older than fourteen to be fingerprinted and registered. They were also required to report changes of address within five days.

Tension between whites and Japanese immigrants in California, which had been building since the beginning of the century, came to a head with the bombing of Pearl Harbor in 1941. Believing that even those Japanese living in the US were likely to be loyal to their native country, the president ordered numerous Japanese to be arrested on suspicion of subversive action and isolated in exclusion zones known as War Relocation Camps. Approximately 120,000 Japanese-Americans, two-thirds of them US citizens, were sent to these camps during the war.

General state of the US after World War II

Following WWII, the US became the strongest political power in the world, becoming a major player in world affairs and foreign policies. The US determined to stop the spread of communism, having named itself the "arsenal of democracy" during the war. In addition, America emerged with a greater sense of itself as a single, integrated nation, with many regional and economic differences diminished. The government worked for greater equality and the growth of communications increased contact among different areas of the country. Both the aftermath of the Great Depression and the necessities of WWII had given the government greater control over various institutions as well as the economy. This also meant that the American government took on greater responsibility for the well-being of its citizens, both in the domestic arena, such as providing basic needs, and in protecting them from foreign threats. This increased role of providing basic necessities for all Americans has been criticized by some as "the welfare state."

Harry S. Truman

Harry S. Truman took over the presidency from Franklin D. Roosevelt near the end of WWII. He made the final decision to drop atomic bombs on Japan and played a major role in the final decisions regarding treatment of post-war Germany. On the domestic front, Truman initiated a 21-point plan known as the Fair Deal. This plan expanded Social Security, provided public housing, and made the Fair Employment Practice Committee permanent. Truman helped support Greece and Turkey (which were under threat from the USSR), supported South Korea against communist North Korea, and helped with recovery in Western Europe. He also participated in the formation of NATO, the North Atlantic Treaty Organization.

Korean War

The Korean War began in 1950 and ended in 1953. For the first time in history, a world organization—the United Nations—played a military role in a war. North Korea sent communist troops into South Korea, seeking to bring the entire country under communist control. The UN sent out a call to member nations, asking them to support South Korea. Truman sent troops, as did many other UN member nations. The war ended three years later with a truce rather than a peace treaty, and Korea remains divided at the 38th parallel north, with communist rule remaining in the North and a democratic government ruling the South.

Dwight D. Eisenhower

Eisenhower carried out a middle-of-the-road foreign policy and brought the US several steps forward in equal rights. He worked to minimize tensions during the Cold War, and negotiated a peace treaty with Russia after the death of Stalin. He enforced desegregation by sending troops to Little Rock Central High School in Arkansas, as well as ordering the desegregation of the military. Organizations formed during his administration included the Department of Health, Education and Welfare, and the National Aeronautics and Space Administration (NASA).

John F. Kennedy

Although his term was cut short by his assassination, JFK instituted economic programs that led to a period of continuous expansion in the US unmatched since before WWII. He formed the Alliance for Progress and the Peace Corps, organizations intended to help developing nations. He also oversaw the passage of new civil rights legislation, and drafted plans to attack poverty and its causes, along with support of the arts. Kennedy's presidency ended when he was assassinated by Lee Harvey Oswald in 1963.

Cuban Missile Crisis

The Cuban Missile Crisis occurred in 1962, during John F. Kennedy's presidency. Russian Premier Nikita Khrushchev decided to place nuclear missiles in Cuba to protect the island from invasion by the US. An American U-2 plane flying over the island photographed the missile bases as they were being built. Tensions rose, with the US concerned about nuclear missiles so close to its shores, and the USSR concerned about American missiles that had been placed in Turkey. Eventually, the missile sites were removed, and a US naval blockade turned back Soviet ships carrying missiles to Cuba. During negotiations, the US agreed to remove their missiles from Turkey and agreed to sell surplus wheat to the USSR. A telephone hotline between Moscow and Washington was set up to allow instant communication between the two heads of state to prevent similar incidents in the future.

Lyndon B. Johnson

Kennedy's Vice President, Lyndon Johnson, assumed the presidency after Kennedy's assassination. He supported civil rights bills, tax cuts, and other wide-reaching legislation that Kennedy had also supported. Johnson saw America as a "Great Society," and enacted legislation to fight disease and poverty, renew urban areas, support education and environmental conservation. Medicare and Medicaid were instituted under his administration. He continued Kennedy's support of space exploration and he is also known, although less positively, for his handling of the Vietnam War.

Civil Rights Movement

In the 1950s, post-war America was experiencing a rapid growth in prosperity. However, African-Americans found themselves left behind. Following the lead of Mahatma Gandhi, who led similar class struggles in India, African-Americans began to demand equal rights. Major figures in this struggle included:
- Rosa Parks—often called the "mother of the Civil Rights Movement," her refusal to give up her seat on the bus to a white man served as a seed from which the movement grew.
- Martin Luther King, Jr.—the best-known leader of the movement, King drew on Gandhi's beliefs and encouraged non-violent opposition. He led a march on Washington in 1963, received the Nobel Peace Prize in 1964, and was assassinated in 1968.
- Malcolm X—espousing less peaceful means of change, Malcolm X became a Black Muslim, and supported black nationalism.
- Stokely Carmichael—Carmichael originated the term "Black Power" and served as head of the Student Nonviolent Coordinating Committee. He believed in black pride and black culture, and felt separate political and social institutions should be developed for blacks.
- Adam Clayton Powell—chairman of the Coordinating Committee for Employment, he led rent strikes and other actions, as well as a bus boycott, to increase the hiring of blacks.
- Jesse Jackson—Jackson was selected to head the Chicago Operation Breadbasket in 1966, and went on to organize boycotts and other actions. He also had an unsuccessful run for President.

Three major events of the Civil Rights Movement are:
- Montgomery Bus Boycott—in 1955, Rosa Parks refused to give her seat on the bus to a white man. As a result, she was tried and convicted of disorderly conduct and of violating local ordinances. A 381-day bus boycott ensued, protesting segregation on public buses.
- Desegregation of Little Rock—in 1957, after the Supreme Court decision on Brown v. Board of Education, which declared "separate but equal" unconstitutional, the Arkansas school board voted to desegregate their schools. Even though Arkansas was considered progressive, its governor brought in the Arkansas National Guard to prevent nine black students from entering Central High School in Little Rock. President Eisenhower responded by federalizing the National Guard and ordering them to stand down.
- Birmingham Campaign—protestors organized a variety of actions such as sit-ins and an organized march to launch a voting campaign. When the City of Birmingham declared the protests illegal, the protestors, including Martin Luther King, Jr., persisted and were arrested and jailed.

Three major pieces of legislation passed as a result of the Civil Rights movement are:
- Brown v. Board of Education (1954)—the Supreme Court declared that "separate but equal" accommodations and services were unconstitutional.
- Civil Rights Act of 1964—this declared discrimination illegal in employment, education, or public accommodation.
- Voting Rights Act of 1965—this act ended various activities practiced, mostly in the South, to bar blacks from exercising their voting rights. These included poll taxes and literacy tests.

Vietnam War

After World War II, the US pledged, as part of its foreign policy, to come to the assistance of any country threatened by communism. When Vietnam was divided into a communist North and democratic South, much like Korea before it, the eventual attempts by the North to unify the country under Communist rule led to intervention by the US. On the home front, the Vietnam War became more and more unpopular politically, with Americans growing increasingly discontent with the inability of the US to achieve the goals it had set for the Asian country. When President Richard Nixon took office in 1969, his escalation of the war led to protests at Kent State in Ohio, during which several students were killed by National Guard troops. Protests continued, eventually resulting in the end of the compulsory draft in 1973. In that same year, the US departed Vietnam. In 1975, the south surrendered, and Vietnam became a unified country under communist rule.

US Cold War foreign policy acts

The following are US Cold War foreign policy acts and how they affected international relationships, especially between the US and the Soviet Union:
- Marshall Plan—this sent aid to war-torn Europe after WWII, largely focusing on preventing the spread of communism.
- Containment Policy—proposed by George F. Kennan, the containment policy focused on containing the spread of Soviet communism.

- Truman Doctrine—Harry S. Truman stated that the US would provide both economic and military support to any country threatened by Soviet takeover.
- National Security Act—passed in 1947, this act reorganized the government's military departments into the Department of Defense, as well as creating the Central Intelligence Agency and the National Security Council. *CIA + NSC*

The combination of these acts led to the Cold War, with Soviet communists attempting to spread their influence and the US and other countries trying to contain or stop this spread.

> **Review Video:** The Cold War: The United States and Russia
> *Visit **mometrix.com/academy** and enter **Code:** **981433***

NATO, the Warsaw Pact, and the Berlin Wall

NATO, the North Atlantic Treaty Organization, came into being in 1949. It essentially amounted to an agreement among the US and Western European countries that an attack on any one of these countries was to be considered an attack against the entire group.

Under the influence of the Soviet Union, the Eastern European countries of the USSR, Bulgaria, East Germany, Poland, Romania, Albania, Hungary, and Czechoslovakia responded with the Warsaw Pact, which created a similar agreement among those nations. In 1961, a wall was built to separate communist East Berlin from democratic West Berlin. This was a literal representation of the "Iron Curtain" that separated the democratic and communist countries through the world.

Arms race

After World War II, major nations, particularly the US and USSR, rushed to develop highly advanced weapons systems such as the atomic bomb and later the hydrogen bomb. These countries seemed determined to outpace each other with the development of numerous, deadly weapons. These weapons were expensive and extremely dangerous, and it is possible that the war between US and Soviet interests remained "cold" due to the fear that one side or the other would use these powerful weapons.

End of the Cold War

In the late 1980s, Mikhail Gorbachev led the Soviet Union. He introduced a series of reform programs. Ronald Reagan famously urged Gorbachev to tear down the Berlin Wall as a gesture of growing freedom in the Eastern Bloc, and in 1989 it was demolished, ending the separation of East and West Germany. The Soviet Union relinquished its power over the various republics in Eastern Europe, and they became independent nations with their own individual governments. In 1991, the USSR was dissolved and the Cold War also came to an end.

> **Review Video:** The Cold War: Resolution
> *Visit **mometrix.com/academy** and enter **Code:** **843092***

Technological advances after WWII

Numerous technological advances after the Second World War led to more effective treatment of diseases, more efficient communication and transportation, and new means of generating power. Advances in medicine increased the human lifespan in developed countries, and near-instantaneous communication opened up a myriad of possibilities. Some of these advances include:
- Discovery of penicillin (1928)
- Supersonic air travel (1947)
- Nuclear power plants (1951)
- Orbital satellite leading to manned space flight (Sputnik, 1957)
- First man on the moon (1969)

US policy toward immigrants after World War II

Prior to WWII, the US had been limiting immigration for several decades. After WWII, policy shifted slightly to accommodate political refugees from Europe and elsewhere. So many people were displaced by the war that in 1946, the UN formed the International Refugee Organization to deal with the problem. In 1948, the US Congress passed the Displaced Persons Act, which allowed over 400,000 European refugees to enter the US, most of them concentration camp survivors and refugees from Eastern Europe.

In 1952, the United States Escapee Program (USEP) increased the quotas, allowing refugees from communist Europe to enter the US, as did the Refugee Relief Act, passed in 1953. At the same time, however, the Internal Security Act of 1950 allowed deportation of declared communists, and Asians were subjected to a quota based on race, rather than country of origin. Later changes included:
- Migration and Refugee Assistance Act (1962)—provided aid for refugees in need
- Immigration and Nationality Act (1965)—ended quotas based on nation of origin
- Immigration Reform and Control Act (1986)—prohibited the hiring of illegal immigrants, but also granted amnesty to about three million illegals already in the country

Expansion of minority rights

Several major acts have been passed, particularly since WWII, to protect the rights of minorities in America. These include:
- Civil Rights Act (1964)
- Voting Rights Act (1965)
- Age Discrimination Act (1967)
- Americans with Disabilities Act (1990)

Other important movements for civil rights included a prisoner's rights movement, movements for immigrant rights, and the women's rights movement. The National Organization for Women (NOW) was established in 1966 and worked to pass the Equal Rights Amendment. The amendment was passed, but not enough states ratified it for it to become part of the US Constitution.

Richard Nixon (R, 1969-1974)

Richard Nixon is best known for the Watergate scandal during his presidency, but other important events marked his tenure as president, including:
- End of the Vietnam War
- Improved diplomatic relations between the US and China, and the US and the USSR
- National Environmental Policy Act passed, providing for environmental protection
- Compulsory draft ended
- Supreme Court legalized abortion in Roe v. Wade
- Watergate

The Watergate scandal of 1972 ended Nixon's presidency. Rather than face impeachment and removal from office, he resigned in 1974.

Gerald Ford (R, 1974-1977)

Gerald Ford was appointed to the vice presidency after Nixon's vice president Spiro Agnew resigned in 1973 under charges of tax evasion. With Nixon's resignation, Ford became president.

Ford's presidency saw negotiations with Russia to limit nuclear arms, as well as struggles to deal with inflation, economic downturn, and energy shortages. Ford's policies sought to reduce governmental control of various businesses and reduce the role of government overall. He also worked to prevent escalation of conflicts in the Middle East.

Jimmy Carter (D, 1977-1981)

Jimmy Carter was elected as president in 1976. Faced with a budget deficit, high unemployment, and continued inflation, Carter also dealt with numerous matters of international diplomacy including:
- Torrijos-Carter Treaties—the US gave control of the Panama Canal to Panama.
- Camp David Accords—negotiations between Anwar el-Sadat, the president of Egypt, and Menachem Begin, the Israeli Prime Minister, led to a peace treaty between Egypt and Israel.
- Strategic Arms Limitation Talks (SALT)—these led to agreements and treaties between the US and the Soviet Union.
- Iran Hostage Crisis—after the Shah of Iran was deposed, an Islamic cleric, Ayatollah Khomeini, came to power. The shah came to the US for medical treatment and Iran demanded his return so he could stand trial. In retaliation, a group of Iranian students stormed the US Embassy in Iran. Fifty-two American hostages were held for 444 days.

Jimmy Carter was awarded the Nobel Peace Prize in 2002.

- 42 -

Ronald Reagan (R, 1981-1989)

Ronald Reagan, at 69, became the oldest American president. The two terms of his administration included notable events such as:
- Reaganomics, also known as supply-side, trickle-down, or free-market economics, involving major tax cuts
- Economic Recovery Tax Act of 1981
- First female justice appointed to the Supreme Court—Sandra Day O'Connor
- Massive increase in the national debt – from $1 trillion to $3 trillion
- Reduction of nuclear weapons via negotiations with Mikhail Gorbachev
- Iran-Contra scandal—cover-up of US involvement in revolutions in El Salvador and Nicaragua
- Deregulation of savings and loan industry
- Loss of the space shuttle *Challenger*

George H. W. Bush (R, 1989-1993)

Reagan's presidency was followed by a term under his former Vice President, George H. W. Bush. Bush's run for president included the famous "thousand points of light" speech, which was instrumental in increasing his standing in the election polls. During Bush's presidency, numerous international events took place, including:
- Fall of the Berlin wall and Germany's unification
- Panamanian dictator Manuel Noriega captured and tried on drug and racketeering charges
- Dissolution of the Soviet Union
- Gulf War, or Operation Desert Storm, triggered by Iraq's invasion of Kuwait
- Tiananmen Square Massacre in Beijing, China
- Ruby Ridge
- The arrival of the World Wide Web

Bill Clinton (D, 1993-2001)

William Jefferson "Bill" Clinton was the second president in US history to be impeached, but he was not convicted, and maintained high approval ratings in spite of the impeachment. Major events during his presidency included:
- Family and Medical Leave Act
- Don't Ask, Don't Tell, a compromise position regarding homosexuals serving in the military
- North American Free Trade Agreement, or NAFTA
- Defense of Marriage Act
- Oslo Accords
- Siege at Waco, Texas, involving the Branch Davidians led by David Koresh
- Bombing of the Murrah Federal Building in Oklahoma City, Oklahoma
- Troops sent to Haiti, Bosnia and Somalia to assist with domestic problems in those areas

George W. Bush (R, 2001-2009)

George W. Bush, son of George Herbert Walker Bush, became president after Clinton. Major events during his presidency included:
- September 11, 2001, al-Qaeda terrorists hijack commercial airliners and fly into the World Trade Center towers and the Pentagon, killing nearly 3000 Americans
- US troops sent to Afghanistan to hunt down al-Qaeda leaders, including the head of the organization, Osama Bin Laden; beginning of the War on Terror
- US troops sent to Iraq, along with a multinational coalition, to depose Saddam Hussein and prevent his deployment of suspected weapons of mass destruction
- Subprime mortgage crisis and near collapse of the financial industry, leading to the Great Recession; first of multiple government bailouts of the financial industry

Barack Obama (D, 2009-2017)

Barack Obama, a first-term senator from Illinois, became the first African-American president. Major events included:
- Multiple bailout packages and spending efforts, in an attempt to inject more money into a stagnant economy
- Massive increase in the national debt – from $10 trillion to $18 trillion
- Reinforcement of the War on Terror in Afghanistan and Iraq; additional deployment of troops in Libya and Syria
- Capture and execution of Osama Bin Laden
- Passage of the Affordable Care Act, legislation that greatly increased government involvement in the healthcare industry, and required every person living in the US to maintain health insurance coverage
- Moves to broaden gay rights, including the repeal of Clinton's Don't Ask, Don't Tell policy for homosexuals serving in the military

Donald Trump (R, 2017-)

Donald Trump, a billionaire real estate tycoon with no prior political experience, was elected to the presidency in a surprise victory over former First Lady and Secretary of State (under Obama) Hillary Clinton. His platform focused on increasing immigration enforcement to curb illegal immigration, restricting foreign trade to improve the dwindling American manufacturing industry, and repealing the Affordable Care Act passed during the prior administration.

World History

Prehistory

Prehistory is the period of human history before writing was developed. The three major periods of prehistory are:

- Lower Paleolithic—Humans used crude tools.
- Upper Paleolithic—Humans began to develop a wider variety of tools. These tools were better made and more specialized. They also began to wear clothes, organize in groups with definite social structures, and to practice art. Most lived in caves during this time period.
- Neolithic—Social structures became even more complex, including growth of a sense of family and the ideas of religion and government. Humans learned to domesticate animals and produce crops, build houses, start fires with friction tools, and to knit, spin and weave.

Anthropology

Anthropology is the study of human culture. Anthropologists study groups of humans, how they relate to each other, and the similarities and differences between these different groups and cultures. Anthropological research takes two approaches: cross-cultural research and comparative research. Most anthropologists work by living among different cultures and participating in those cultures in order to learn about them.

There are four major divisions within anthropology:

- Biological anthropology
- Cultural anthropology
- Linguistic anthropology
- Archaeology

Archeology

Archeology studies past human cultures by evaluating what they leave behind. This can include bones, buildings, art, tools, pottery, graves, and even trash. Archeologists maintain detailed notes and records of their findings and use special tools to evaluate what they find. Photographs, notes, maps, artifacts, and surveys of the area can all contribute to evaluation of an archeological site. By studying all these elements of numerous archeological sites, scientists have been able to theorize that humans or near-humans have existed for about 600,000 years. Before that, more primitive humans are believed to have appeared about one million years ago. These humans eventually developed into Cro-Magnon man, and then Homo sapiens, or modern man.

Human development from the Lower Paleolithic to the Iron Age

Human development has been divided into several phases:
- Lower Paleolithic or Early Stone Age, beginning two to three million years ago—early humans used tools like needles, hatchets, awls, and cutting tools.
- Middle Paleolithic or Middle Stone Age, beginning approximately 300,000 B.C.E.—sophisticated stone tools were developed, along with hunting, gathering, and ritual practices.
- Upper Paleolithic or Late Stone Age, beginning approximately 40,000 B.C.E.—including the Mesolithic and Neolithic eras, textiles and pottery are developed. Humans of this era discovered the wheel, began to practice agriculture, made polished tools, and had some domesticated animals.
- Bronze Age, beginning in approximately 3,000 B.C.E.—metals are discovered and the first civilizations emerge as humans become more technologically advanced.
- Iron Age, beginning in 1,200 to 1,000 B.C.E.—metal tools replace stone tools as humans develop knowledge of smelting.

Civilizations

Civilizations are defined as having the following characteristics:
- Use of metal to make weapons and tools
- Written language
- A defined territorial state
- A calendar

The earliest civilizations developed in river valleys where reliable, fertile land was easily found, including:
- The Nile River Valley in Egypt
- Mesopotamia
- The Indus Valley
- Hwang Ho in China

The very earliest civilizations developed in the Tigris-Euphrates valley in Mesopotamia, which is now part of Iraq, and in Egypt's Nile valley. These civilizations arose between 5,000 and 3,000 B.C.E. The area where these civilizations grew is known as the Fertile Crescent. Geography and the availability of water made large-scale human habitation possible.

Importance of rivers and water
The earliest civilizations are also referred to as fluvial civilizations because they were founded near rivers. Rivers and the water they provide were vital to these early groupings, offering:
- Water for drinking, cultivating crops, and caring for domesticated animals
- A gathering place for wild animals that could be hunted
- Rich soil deposits as a result of regular flooding

Irrigation techniques helped direct water where it was most needed, to sustain herds of domestic animals and to nourish crops of increasing size and quality.

Fertile Crescent

James Breasted, an archeologist from the University of Chicago, popularized the term "Fertile Crescent" to describe the area in the Near East where the earliest civilizations arose. The region includes modern day Iraq, Syria, Lebanon, Israel, Palestine, and Jordan. It is bordered on the south by the Syrian and Arabian Deserts, the west by the Mediterranean Sea, and to the north and east by the Taurus and Zagros Mountains respectively. This area not only provided the raw materials for the development of increasingly advanced civilizations, but also saw waves of migration and invasion, leading to the earliest wars and genocides as groups conquered and absorbed each other's cultures and inhabitants.

Egyptian, Sumerian, Babylonian, and Assyrian cultures

The Egyptians were one of the most advanced ancient cultures, having developed construction methods to build the great pyramids, as well as a form of writing known as hieroglyphics. Their religion was highly developed and complex, and included advanced techniques for the preservation of bodies after death. They also made paper by processing papyrus, a plant commonly found along the Nile, invented the decimal system, devised a solar calendar, and advanced overall knowledge of mathematics.

> ➤ **Review Video:** Egyptians
> *Visit **mometrix.com/academy** and enter **Code**: **152695***

The Sumerians were the first to invent the wheel, and also brought irrigation systems into use. Their cuneiform writing was simpler than Egyptian hieroglyphs, and they developed the timekeeping system we still use today.

> ➤ **Review Video:** Early Mesopotamia: The Sumerians
> *Visit **mometrix.com/academy** and enter **Code**: **987440***

The Babylonians are best known for the Code of Hammurabi, an advanced law code.

> ➤ **Review Video:** Early Mesopotamia: The Babylonians
> *Visit **mometrix.com/academy** and enter **Code**: **340325***

The Assyrians developed horse-drawn chariots and an organized military.

Hebrew, Persian, Minoan, and Mycenaean cultures

The Hebrew or ancient Israelite culture developed the monotheistic religion that eventually developed into modern Judaism and Christianity.

The Persians were conquerors, but those they conquered were allowed to keep their own laws, customs, and religious traditions rather than being forced to accept those of their conquerors. They also developed an alphabet and practiced Zoroastrianism and Mithraism, religions that have influenced modern religious practice.

The Minoans used a syllabic writing system and built large, colorful palaces. These ornate buildings included sewage systems, running water, bathtubs, and even flushing toilets. Their script, known as Linear A, has yet to be deciphered.

The Mycenaeans practiced a religion that grew into the Greek pantheon, worshipping Zeus and other Olympian gods. They developed Linear B, a writing system used to write the earliest known form of Greek.

Phoenicians and early culture in India and ancient China

Skilled seafarers and navigators, the Phoenicians used the stars to navigate their ships at night. They developed a purple dye that was in great demand in the ancient world, and worked with glass and metals. They also devised a phonetic alphabet, using symbols to represent individual sounds rather than whole words or syllables.

In the Indus Valley, an urban civilization arose in what is now India. These ancient humans developed the concept of zero in mathematics, practiced an early form of the Hindu religion, and developed the caste system which is still prevalent in India today. Archeologists are still uncovering information about this highly developed ancient civilization.

In ancient China, human civilization developed along the Yangtze River. These people produced silk, grew millet, and made pottery, including Longshan black pottery.

Civilizations of Mesopotamia

The major civilizations of Mesopotamia, in what is now called the Middle East, were:
- Sumerians
- Amorites
- Hittites
- Assyrians
- Chaldeans
- Persians

These cultures controlled different areas of Mesopotamia during various time periods, but were similar in that they were autocratic: a single ruler served as the head of the government and often was the main religious ruler as well. These rulers were often tyrannical, militaristic leaders who controlled all aspects of life, including law, trade, and religious activity. Portions of the legacies of these civilizations remain in cultures today. These include mythologies, religious systems, mathematical innovations and even elements of various languages.

Sumer

Sumer, located in the southern part of Mesopotamia, consisted of a dozen city-states. Each city-state had its own gods, and the leader of each city-state also served as the high priest. Cultural legacies of Sumer include:
- The invention of writing
- Invention of the wheel
- The first library—established in Assyria by Ashurbanipal

- The Hanging Gardens of Babylon—one of the Seven Wonders of the Ancient World
- First written laws—Ur-Nammu's Codes and the Codes of Hammurabi
- The *Epic of Gilgamesh*—the first recorded epic story

Kushite culture

Kush, or Cush, was located in Nubia, south of ancient Egypt, and the earliest existing records of this civilization were found in Egyptian texts. At one time, Kush was the largest empire on the Nile River, ruling not only Nubia but Upper and Lower Egypt as well.

In Neolithic times, Kushites lived in villages, with buildings made of mud bricks. They were settled rather than nomadic, and practiced hunting and fishing, cultivated grain, and also herded cattle. Kerma, the capital, was a major center of trade.

Kush determined leadership through matrilineal descent of their kings, as did Egypt. Their heads of state, the Kandake or Kentake, were female. Their polytheistic religion included the primary Egyptian gods as well as regional gods, including a lion-headed god, which is commonly found in African cultures.

Archeological evidence indicates the Kushites were a mix of Mediterranean and Negroid peoples. Kush was conquered by the Aksumite Empire in the 4th century CE.

Minoan civilization

The Minoans lived on the island of Crete, just off the coast of Greece. This civilization reigned from approximately 4000 to 1400 B.C.E. and is considered to be the first advanced civilization in Europe. The Minoans developed writing systems known to linguists as Linear A and Linear B. Linear A has not yet been translated; Linear B evolved into classical Greek script. "Minoans" is not the name they used for themselves, but is instead a variation on the name of King Minos, a king in Greek mythology believed by some to have been a denizen of Crete. The Minoan civilization subsisted on trade, and their way of life was often disrupted by earthquakes and volcanoes. Much is still unknown about the Minoans, and archeologists continue to study their architecture and archeological remains. The Minoan culture eventually fell to Greek invaders and was supplanted by the Mycenaean civilization.

Influences of ancient Indian civilization

The civilizations of ancient India gave rise to both Hinduism and Buddhism, major world religions that have influenced countries far from their place of origin. Practices such as yoga, increasingly popular in the West, can trace their roots to these earliest Indian civilizations, and the poses are still formally referred to by Sanskrit names. Literature from ancient India includes the *Mahabharata* containing the *Bhagavad Gita*, the *Ramayana*, *Arthashastra*, and the *Vedas*, a collection of sacred texts. Indo-European languages, including English, find their beginnings in these ancient cultures. Ancient Indo-Aryan languages such as Sanskrit are still used in some formal Hindu practices.

Earliest civilizations in China

Many historians believe Chinese civilization is the oldest uninterrupted civilization in the world. The Neolithic age in China goes back to 10,000 B.C.E., with agriculture in China beginning as early as 5,000 B.C.E. Their system of writing dates to 1,500 B.C.E. The Yellow River served as the center for the earliest Chinese settlements. In Ningxia, in northwest China, there are carvings on cliffs that date back to the Paleolithic Period, indicating the extreme antiquity of Chinese culture. Literature from ancient China includes Confucius' *Analects*, the *Tao Te Ching*, and a variety of poetry.

Ancient American cultures

Less is known of ancient American civilizations since less was left behind. Some of the more well-known cultures include:
- The Norte Chico civilization in Peru, an agricultural society of up to 30 individual communities, existed over 5,000 years ago. This culture is also known as the Caral-Supe civilization, and is the oldest known civilization in the Americas.
- The Anasazi, or Ancestral Pueblo People, lived in what is now the southwestern United States. Emerging about 1200 B.C.E., the Anasazi built complex adobe dwellings and were the forerunners of later Pueblo Indian cultures.
- The Maya emerged in southern Mexico and northern Central America as early as 2,600 B.C.E. They developed a written language and a complex calendar.

> **Review Video:** American Civilizations: Early Cultures
> *Visit mometrix.com/academy and enter Code:* **575452**

> **Review Video:** American Civilizations: The Mayas
> *Visit mometrix.com/academy and enter Code:* **556527**

Mycenaean civilization

In contrast to the Minoans, whom they displaced, the Mycenaeans relied more on conquest than on trade. Mycenaean states included Sparta, Athens, and Corinth. The history of this civilization, including the Trojan War, was recorded by the Greek poet, Homer. His work was largely considered mythical until archeologists discovered evidence of the city of Troy in Hisarlik, Turkey. Archeologists continue to add to the body of information about this ancient culture, translating documents written in Linear B, a script derived from the Minoan Linear A. It is theorized that the Mycenaean civilization was eventually destroyed in either a Dorian invasion or an attack by Greek invaders from the north.

Dorian invasion

A Dorian invasion does not refer to an invasion by a particular group of people, but rather is a hypothetical theory to explain the end of the Mycenaean civilization and the growth of classical Greece. Ancient tradition refers to these events as "the return of the Heracleidae," or the sons (descendents) of Hercules. Archeologists and historians still do not know exactly who conquered the Mycenaeans, but it is believed to have occurred around 1200 B.C.E., contemporaneous with the destruction of the Hittite civilization in what is now modern Turkey. The Hittites speak of an attack by people of the Aegean Sea, or the "Sea People." Only Athens was left intact.

Spartans and Athenians

Both powerful city-states, Sparta and Athens fought each other in the Peloponnesian War (431-404 B.C.E.). Despite their proximity, the Spartans and the Athenians nurtured contrasting cultures:

- The Spartans, located in Peloponnesus, were ruled by an oligarchic military state. They practiced farming, disallowed trade for Spartan citizens, and valued military arts and strict discipline. They emerged as the strongest military force in the area, and maintained this status for many years. In one memorable encounter, a small group of Spartans held off a huge army of Persians at Thermopylae.
- The Athenians were centered in Attica, where the land was rocky and unsuitable for farming. Like the Spartans, they descended from invaders who spoke Greek. Their government was very different from Sparta's; it was in Athens that democracy was created by Cleisthenes of Athens in 508 B.C.E. Athenians excelled in art, theater, architecture, and philosophy.

Contributions of ancient Greece

Ancient Greece made numerous major contributions to cultural development, including:

- Theater—Aristophanes and other Greek playwrights laid the groundwork for modern theatrical performance.
- Alphabet—the Greek alphabet, derived from the Phoenician alphabet, developed into the Roman alphabet, and then into our modern-day alphabet.
- Geometry—Pythagoras and Euclid pioneered much of the system of geometry still taught today. Archimedes made various mathematical discoveries, including calculating a very accurate value of pi.
- Historical writing—much of ancient history doubles as mythology or religious texts. Herodotus and Thucydides made use of research and interpretation to record historical events.
- Philosophy—Socrates, Plato, and Aristotle served as the fathers of Western philosophy. Their work is still required reading for philosophy students.

Alexander the Great

Born to Philip II of Macedon and tutored by Aristotle, Alexander the Great is considered one of the greatest conquerors in history. He conquered Egypt, the Achaemenid/Persian Empire, a powerful empire founded by Cyrus the Great that spanned three continents, and he traveled as far as India and the Iberian Peninsula. Though Alexander died from malaria at age 32, his conquering efforts spread Greek culture into the east. This cultural diffusion left a greater mark on history than did his empire, which fell apart due to internal conflict not long after his death. Trade between the East and West increased, as did an exchange of ideas and beliefs that influenced both regions greatly. The Hellenistic traditions his conquest spread were prevalent in Byzantine culture until as late as the 15th century.

Hittite Empire

The Hittites were centered in what is now Turkey, but their empire extended into Palestine and Syria. They conquered the Babylonian civilization, but adopted their religion, laws, and literature. Overall, the Hittites tended to tolerate other religions, unlike many other contemporary cultures, and absorbed foreign gods into their own belief systems rather than

- 51 -

forcing their religion onto peoples they conquered. The Hittite Empire reached its peak in 1600-1200 B.C.E. After a war with Egypt, which weakened them severely, they were eventually conquered by the Assyrians.

Persian Wars

The Persian Empire, ruled by Cyrus the Great, encompassed an area from the Black Sea to Afghanistan, and beyond into Central Asia. After the death of Cyrus, Darius I became king in 522 B.C.E. The empire reached its zenith during his reign and Darius attempted to conquer Greece as well. From 499-449 B.C.E., the Greeks and Persians fought in the Persian Wars. The Peace of Callias brought an end to the fighting, after the Greeks were able to repel the invasion.

Battles of the Persian Wars included:
- The Battle of Marathon—heavily outnumbered Greek forces managed to achieve victory.
- The Battle of Thermopylae—a small band of Spartans held off a throng of Persian troops for several days before Persia defeated the Greeks and captured an evacuated Athens.
- The Battle of Salamis—this was a naval battle that again saw outnumbered Greeks achieving victory.
- The Battle of Plataea—this was another Greek victory, but one in which they outnumbered the Persians. This ended the invasion of Greece.

Maurya Empire

The Maurya Empire was a large, powerful empire established in India. It was one of the largest ever to rule in the Indian subcontinent, and existed from 322 to 185 B.C.E., ruled by Chandragupta Maurya after the withdrawal from India of Alexander the Great. The Maurya Empire was highly developed, including a standardized economic system, waterways, and private corporations. Trade to the Greeks and others became common, with goods including silk, exotic foods, and spices. Religious development included the rise of Buddhism and Jainism. The laws of the Maurya Empire protected not only civil and social rights of the citizens, but also protected animals, establishing protected zones for economically important creatures such as elephants, lions and tigers. This period of time in Indian history was largely peaceful, perhaps due to the strong Buddhist beliefs of many of its leaders. The empire finally fell after a succession of weak leaders, and was taken over by Demetrius, a Greco-Bactrian king who took advantage of this lapse in leadership to conquer southern Afghanistan and Pakistan around 180 B.C.E., forming the Indo-Greek Kingdom.

Chinese dynasties

In China, history was divided into a series of dynasties. The most famous of these, the Han dynasty, existed from 206 B.C.E. to 220 CE. Accomplishments of the Chinese Empires included:
- Building the Great Wall of China
- Numerous inventions, including paper, paper money, printing, and gunpowder
- High level of artistic development
- Silk production

The Chinese dynasties were comparable to Rome as far as their artistic and intellectual accomplishments, as well as the size and scope of their influence.

Roman Republic and Empire

Rome began humbly, in a single town that grew out of Etruscan settlements and traditions, founded, according to legend, by twin brothers Romulus and Remus, who were raised by wolves. Romulus killed Remus, and from his legacy grew Rome. A thousand years later, the Roman Empire covered a significant portion of the known world, from what is now Scotland, across Europe, and into the Middle East. Hellenization, or the spread of Greek culture throughout the world, served as an inspiration and a model for the spread of Roman culture. Rome brought in belief systems of conquered peoples as well as their technological and scientific accomplishments, melding the disparate parts into a Roman core. Rome began as a republic ruled by consuls, but after the assassination of Julius Caesar, it became an empire led by emperors. Rome's overall government was autocratic, but local officials came from the provinces where they lived. This limited administrative system was probably a major factor in the long life of the empire.

Byzantine Empire

In the early fourth century, the Roman Empire split, with the eastern portion becoming the Eastern Empire, or the Byzantine Empire. In 330 CE, Constantine founded the city of Constantinople, which became the center of the Byzantine Empire. Its major influences came from Mesopotamia and Persia, in contrast to the Western Empire, which maintained traditions more closely linked to Greece and Carthage. Byzantium's position gave it an advantage over invaders from the west and the east, as well as control over trade from both regions. It protected the Western empire from invasion from the Persians and the Ottomans, and practiced a more centralized rule than in the West. The Byzantines were famous for lavish art and architecture, as well as the Code of Justinian, which collected Roman law into a clear system. The Byzantine Empire finally fell to the Ottomans in 1453.

Nicene Creed

The Byzantine Empire was Christian-based but incorporated Greek language, philosophy and literature and drew its law and government policies from Rome. However, there was as yet no unified doctrine of Christianity, as it was a relatively new religion that had spread rapidly and without a great deal of organization. In 325, the First Council of Nicaea addressed this issue. From this conference came the Nicene Creed, addressing the Trinity and other basic Christian beliefs. The Council of Chalcedon in 451 further defined the view of the Trinity.

Fall of the Western Roman Empire

Germanic tribes, including the Visigoths, Ostrogoths, Vandals, Saxons and Franks, controlled most of Europe. The Roman Empire faced major opposition on that front. The increasing size of the empire also made it harder to manage, leading to dissatisfaction throughout the empire as Roman government became less efficient. Germanic tribes refused to adhere to the Nicene Creed, instead following Arianism, which led the Roman Catholic Church to declare them heretics. The Franks proved a powerful military force in their defeat of the Muslims in 732. In 768, Charlemagne became king of the Franks. These tribes waged several wars against Rome, including the invasion of Britannia by the Angles and Saxons. Far-flung Rome lost control over this area of its Empire, and eventually Rome itself was invaded.

Iconoclasm and conflict between Roman Catholic and Eastern Orthodox churches

Emperor Leo III ordered the destruction of all icons throughout the Byzantine Empire. Images of Jesus were replaced with crosses, and images of Jesus, Mary or other religious figures were considered blasphemy on grounds of idolatry. Pope Gregory II, called a synod to discuss the issue. The synod declared that the images were not heretical, and that strong disciplinary measures would result for anyone who destroyed them. Leo's response was an attempt to kill Pope Gregory, but this plan ended in failure.

Viking invasions

Vikings invaded Northern France in the tenth century, eventually becoming the Normans. Originating in Scandinavia, the Vikings were accomplished seafarers with advanced knowledge of trade routes. With overpopulation plaguing their native lands, they began to travel. From the eighth to the eleventh centuries, they spread throughout Europe, conquering and colonizing. Vikings invaded and colonized England in several waves, including the Anglo-Saxon invasions that displaced Roman control. Their influence remained significant in England, affecting everything from the language of the country to place names and even the government and social structure. By 900, Vikings had settled in Iceland. They proceeded then to Greenland and eventually to North America, arriving in the New World even before the Spanish and British who claimed the lands several centuries later. They also traded with the Byzantine Empire until the eleventh century when their significant level of activity came to an end.

Tenth century events in the West and the East

In Europe, the years 500-1000 CE are largely known as the Dark Ages. In the tenth century, numerous Viking invasions disrupted societies that had been more settled under Roman rule. Vikings settled in Northern France, eventually becoming the Normans. By the eleventh century, Europe would rise again into the High Middle Ages with the beginning of the Crusades.

In China, wars also raged. This led the Chinese to make use of gunpowder for the first time in warfare.

In the Americas, the Mayan Empire was winding down while the Toltec became more prominent. Pueblo Indian culture was also at its zenith.

In the East, the Muslims and the Byzantine Empire were experiencing a significant period of growth and development.

European feudalism in the Middle Ages

A major element of the social and economic life of Europe, feudalism developed as a way to ensure European rulers would have the wherewithal to quickly raise an army when necessary. Vassals swore loyalty and promised to provide military service for lords, who in return offered a fief, or a parcel of land, for them to use to generate their livelihood. Vassals could work the land themselves, have it worked by peasants or serfs—workers who had few rights and were little more than slaves—or grant the fief to someone else. The king legally owned all the land, but in return promised to protect the vassals from invasion and war. Vassals returned a certain percentage of their income to the lords, who in turn passed a portion of their income on to the king. A similar practice was manorialism, in which the feudal system was applied to a self-contained manor. These manors were often owned by the lords who ran them, but were usually included in the same system of loyalty and promises of protection that drove feudalism.

Influence of the Roman Catholic Church

The Roman Catholic Church extended significant influence both politically and economically throughout medieval society. The church supplied education, as there were no established schools or universities. To a large extent, the church had filled a power void left by various invasions throughout the former Roman Empire, leading it to exercise a role that was far more political than religious. Kings were heavily influenced by the Pope and other church officials, and churches controlled large amounts of land throughout Europe.

Black Death

The Black Death, believed to be bubonic plague, most likely came to Europe on fleas carried by rats on sailing vessels. The plague killed more than a third of the entire population of Europe and effectively ended feudalism as a political system. Many who had formerly served as peasants or serfs found different work, as a demand for skilled labor grew. Nation-states grew in power, and in the face of the pandemic, many began to turn away from faith in God and toward the ideals of ancient Greece and Rome for government and other beliefs.

Crusades

The Crusades began in the eleventh century and continued into the fifteenth. The major goal of these various military ventures was to slow the progression of Muslim forces into Europe and to expel them from the Holy Land, where they had taken control of Jerusalem and Palestine. Alexius I, the Byzantine emperor, called for helped from Pope Urban II when Palestine was taken. In 1095, the Pope, hoping to reunite Eastern and Western Christianity, encouraged all Christians to help the cause. Amidst great bloodshed, this Crusade recaptured Jerusalem, but over the next centuries, Jerusalem and other areas of the Holy Land changed hands numerous times. The Second Crusade (1147-1149) consisted of an unsuccessful attempt to retake Damascus. The Third Crusade, under Pope Gregory VIII, attempted to recapture Jerusalem, but failed. The Fourth Crusade, under Pope Innocent III, attempted to come into the Holy Land via Egypt. The Crusades led to greater power for the Pope and the Catholic Church in general and also opened numerous trading and cultural routes between Europe and the East.

Developments through the eleventh century

Politics in India

After the Mauryan dynasty, the Guptas ruled India, maintaining a long period of peace and prosperity in the area. During this time, the Indian people invented the decimal system as well as the concept of zero. They produced cotton and calico, as well as other products in high demand in Europe and Asia, and developed a complex system of medicine. The Gupta Dynasty ended in the sixth century. First the Huns invaded, and then the Hephthalites (an Asian nomadic tribe) destroyed the weakened empire.

In the fourteenth century, Tamerlane, a Muslim who envisioned restoring Genghis Khan's empire, expanded India's borders and founded the Mogul Empire. His grandson Akbar promoted freedom of religion and built a wide-spread number of mosques, forts, and other buildings throughout the country.

<u>Chinese and Japanese governments</u>
After the Mongols, led by Genghis Khan and his grandson Kublai Khan, unified the Mongol Empire, China was led by the Ming Dynasty (1368-1644) and the Manchu (also known as Qing) Dynasty (1644-1912). Both dynasties were isolationist, ending China's interaction with other countries until the eighteenth century. The Ming Dynasty was known for its porcelain, while the Manchus focused on farming and road construction as the population grew.

Japan developed independently of China, but borrowed the Buddhist religion, the Chinese writing system, and other elements of Chinese society. Ruled by the divine emperor, Japan basically functioned on a feudal system led by daimyo, or warlords, and soldiers known as samurai. Japan remained isolationist, not interacting significantly with the rest of the world until the 1800s.

<u>Africa</u>
Much of Africa was uninhabitable, due to the large amount of desert and other inhospitable terrain. Egypt remained important, though most of the northern coast became Muslim as their armies spread through the area. Ghana rose as a trade center in the ninth century, lasting into the twelfth century, primarily trading in gold, which it exchange for Saharan salt. Mali rose somewhat later, with the trade center Timbuktu becoming an important exporter of goods such as iron, leather and tin. Mali also dealt in agricultural trade, becoming one of the most significant trading centers in West Africa. The Muslim religion dominated, and technological advancement was sparse.

African culture was largely defined through migration, as Arab merchants and others settled on the continent, particularly along the east coast. Scholars from the Muslim nations gravitated to Timbuktu, which in addition to its importance in trade, had also become a magnet for those seeking Islamic knowledge and education.

Islam

Born in 570 CE, Muhammad began preaching around 613, leading his followers in a new religion called Islam, which means "submission to God's will." Before this time, the Arabian Peninsula was inhabited largely by Bedouins, nomads who battled amongst each other and lived in tribal organizations. But by the time Muhammad died in 632, most of Arabia had become Muslim to some extent.

Muhammad conquered Mecca, where a temple called the Kaaba had long served as a center of the nomadic religions. He declared this temple the most sacred of Islam, and Mecca as the holy city. His writings became the Koran, or Qur'an, divine revelations he said had been delivered to him by the angel Gabriel.

Muhammad's teachings gave the formerly tribal Arabian people a sense of unity that had not existed in the area before. After his death, the converted Muslims of Arabia conquered a vast territory, creating an empire and bringing advances in literature, technology, science and art as Europe was declining under the scourge of the Black Death. Literature from this period includes the *Arabian Nights* and the *Rubaiyat* of Omar Khayyam.

Later in its development, Islam split into two factions, the Shiite and the Sunni Muslims. Conflict continues today between these groups.

> ➤ **Review Video:** Islam
> *Visit* ***mometrix.com/academy*** *and enter* ***Code***: **228482**

> ➤ **Review Video:** The Islamic Empire
> *Visit* ***mometrix.com/academy*** *and enter* ***Code***: **511181**

Ottoman Empire

By 1400, the Ottomans had grown in power in Anatolia and had begun attempts to take Constantinople. In 1453 they finally conquered the Byzantine capital and renamed it Istanbul. The Ottoman Empire's major strength, much like Rome before it, lay in its ability to unite widely disparate people through religious tolerance. This tolerance, which stemmed from the idea that Muslims, Christians, and Jews were fundamentally related and could coexist, enabled the Ottomans to develop a widely varied culture. They also believed in just laws and just government, with government centered in a monarch, known as the sultan.

Renaissance

Renaissance literally means "rebirth." After the darkness of the Dark Ages and the Black Plague, interest rose again in the beliefs and politics of ancient Greece and Rome. Art, literature, music, science, and philosophy all burgeoned during the Renaissance.

Many of the ideas of the Renaissance began in Florence, Italy, in the fourteenth century, spurred by the Medici family. Education for the upper classes expanded to include law, math, reading, writing, and classical Greek and Roman works. As the Renaissance progressed, the world was presented through art and literature in a realistic way that had never been explored before. This realism drove culture to new heights.

Artists, authors and scientists

Artists of the Renaissance included Leonardo da Vinci, also an inventor, Michelangelo, also an architect, and others who focused on realism in their work. In literature, major contributions came from humanist authors like Petrarch, Erasmus, Sir Thomas More, and Boccaccio, who believed man should focus on reality rather than on the ethereal. Shakespeare, Cervantes and Dante followed in their footsteps, and their works found a wide audience thanks to Gutenberg's development of the printing press.

Scientific developments of the Renaissance included the work of Copernicus, Galileo and Kepler, who challenged the geocentric philosophies of the day by proving that the earth was not the center of the solar system.

> ➢ **Review Video:** Renaissance
> *Visit mometrix.com/academy and enter Code:* **145504**

Reformation

The Reformation consisted of both the Protestant and the Catholic Reformation. The Protestant Reformation rose in Germany when Martin Luther protested abuses of the Catholic Church. John Calvin led the movement in Switzerland, while in England King Henry VIII made use of the Reformation's ideas to further his own political goals. The Catholic Reformation, or Counter-Reformation, occurred in response to the Protestant movement, leading to various changes in the Catholic Church. Some provided wider tolerance of different religious viewpoints, but others actually increased the persecution of those deemed to be heretics.

From a religious standpoint, the Reformation occurred due to abuses by the Catholic Church such as indulgences and dispensations, religious offices being offered up for sale, and an increasingly dissolute clergy. Politically, the Reformation was driven by increased power of various ruling monarchs, who wished to take all power to themselves rather than allowing power to remain with the church. They also had begun to chafe at papal taxes and the church's increasing wealth. The ideas of the Protestant Revolution removed power from the Catholic Church and the Pope himself, playing nicely into the hands of those monarchs, such as Henry VIII, who wanted out from under the church's control.

> ➢ **Review Video:** The Reformation: The Protestants
> *Visit mometrix.com/academy and enter Code:* **604651**

Scientific Revolution

In addition to holding power in the political realm, church doctrine also governed scientific belief. During the Scientific Revolution, astronomers and other scientists began to amass evidence that challenged the church's scientific doctrines. Major figures of the Scientific Revolution included:
- Nicolaus Copernicus—wrote *On the Revolutions of the Celestial Spheres*, arguing that the earth revolved around the sun
- Tycho Brahe—catalogued astronomical observations
- Johannes Kepler—developed laws of planetary motion
- Galileo Galilei—defended the heliocentric theories of Copernicus and Kepler, discovered four moons of Jupiter, and died under house arrest by the church, charged with heresy
- Isaac Newton—discovered gravity, studied optics, calculus and physics, and believed the workings of nature could be studied and proven through observation

> ➢ **Review Video:** The Scientific Revolution
> *Visit mometrix.com/academy and enter Code:* **972197**

Enlightenment

During the Enlightenment, philosophers and scientists began to rely more and more on observation to support their ideas, rather than building on past beliefs, particularly those held by the church. A focus on ethics and logic drove their work. Major philosophers of the Enlightenment included:

- Rene Descartes—he famously wrote, "I think, therefore I am." He believed strongly in logic and rules of observation.
- David Hume—he pioneered empiricism and skepticism, believing that truth could only be found through direct experience, and that what others said to be true was always suspect.
- Immanuel Kant—he believed in self-examination and observation, and that the root of morality lay within human beings.
- Jean-Jacques Rousseau—he developed the idea of the social contract, that government existed by the agreement of the people, and that the government was obligated to protect the people and their basic rights. His ideas influenced John Locke and Thomas Jefferson.

> ➤ **Review Video:** The Enlightenment
> *Visit **mometrix.com/academy** and enter **Code**: **540039***

American Revolution and French Revolution

Both the American and French Revolution came about as a protest against the excesses and overly controlling nature of their respective monarchs. In America, the British colonies had been left mostly to self-govern until the British monarchs began to increase control, spurring the colonies to revolt. In France, the nobility's excesses had led to increasingly difficult economic conditions, with inflation, heavy taxation and food shortages creating great burdens on the lower classes. Both revolutions led to the development of republics to replace the monarchies that were displaced. However, the French Revolution eventually led to the rise of the dictator Napoleon Bonaparte, while the American Revolution produced a working republic from the beginning.

In 1789, King Louis XVI, faced with a huge national debt, convened parliament. The Third Estate, or Commons, a division of the French parliament, then claimed power, and the king's resistance led to the storming of the Bastille, the royal prison. The people established a constitutional monarchy. When King Louis XVI and Marie Antoinette attempted to leave the country, they were executed on the guillotine. From 1793 to 1794, Robespierre and extreme radicals, the Jacobins, instituted a Reign of Terror, executing tens of thousands of nobles as well as anyone considered an enemy of the Revolution. Robespierre was then executed, as well, and the Directory came into power, leading to a temporary return to bourgeois values.

This governing body proved incompetent and corrupt, allowing Napoleon Bonaparte to come to power in 1799, first as a dictator, then as emperor. While the French Revolution threw off the power of a corrupt monarchy, its immediate results were likely not what the original perpetrators of the revolt had intended.

> ➢ **Review Video:** The Revolutionary War
> Visit ***mometrix.com/academy*** *and enter* **Code: 739570**

> ➢ **Review Video:** The French Revolution: Napoleon Bonaparte
> Visit ***mometrix.com/academy*** *and enter* **Code: 876330**

Russian Revolution of 1905

In Russia, rule lay in the hands of the Czars, and the overall structure was feudalistic. Beneath the Czars was a group of rich nobles, landowners whose lands were worked by peasants and serfs. The Russo-Japanese War (1904-1905) made conditions much worse for the lower classes. When peasants demonstrated outside the Czar's Winter Palace, the palace guard fired upon the crowd. The demonstration had been organized by a trade union leader, and after the violent response, many unions as well as political parties blossomed and began to lead numerous strikes. When the economy ground to a halt, Czar Nicholas II signed a document known as the October Manifesto, which established a constitutional monarchy and gave legislative power to parliament. However, he violated the Manifesto shortly thereafter, disbanding parliament and ignoring the civil liberties granted by the Manifesto. This eventually led to the Bolshevik Revolution.

Bolshevik Revolution of 1917

Throughout its modern history, Russia had lagged behind other countries in development. The continued existence of a feudal system, combined with harsh conditions and the overall size of the country, led to massive food shortages and increasingly harsh conditions for the majority of the population. The tyrannical rule of the Czars only made this worse, as did repeated losses in various military conflicts. Increasing poverty, decreasing supplies, and the Czar's violation of the October Manifesto which had given some political power and civil rights to the people finally came to a head with the Bolshevik Revolution.

Major events
A workers' strike in Petrograd in 1917 set the revolutionary wheels in motion when the army sided with the workers. While parliament set up a provisional government made up of nobles, the workers and military joined to form their own governmental system known as soviets, which consisted of local councils elected by the people. The ensuing chaos opened the doors for formerly exiled leaders Vladimir Lenin, Joseph Stalin and Leon Trotsky to move in and gain popular support as well as the support of the Red Guard. Overthrowing parliament, they took power, creating a communist state in Russia. This development led to the spread of communism throughout Eastern Europe and elsewhere, greatly affecting diplomatic policies throughout the world for several decades.

Industrial Revolution

The Industrial Revolution began in Great Britain, bringing coal- and steam-powered machinery into widespread use. Industry began a period of rapid growth with these developments. Goods that had previously been produced in small workshops or even in homes were produced more efficiently and in much larger quantities in factories. Where society had been largely agrarian-based, the focus swiftly shifted to an industrial outlook. As electricity and internal combustion engines replaced coal and steam as energy sources, even more drastic and rapid changes occurred. Western European countries in particular turned to colonialism, taking control of portions of Africa and Asia to ensure access to the raw materials needed to produce factory goods. Specialized labor became very much in demand, and businesses grew rapidly, creating monopolies, increasing world trade, and developing large urban centers. Even agriculture changed fundamentally as the Industrial Revolution led to a second Agricultural Revolution with the addition of new technology to advance agricultural production.

> ➤ **Review Video:** The Industrial Revolution
> *Visit **mometrix.com/academy** and enter Code:* **258668**

First and second phases
The first phase of the Industrial Revolution took place from roughly 1750 to 1830. The textile industry experienced major changes as more and more elements of the process became mechanized. Mining benefited from the steam engine. Transportation became easier and more widely available as waterways were improved and the railroad came into prominence. In the second phase, from 1830 to 1910, industries further improved in efficiency and new industries were introduced as photography, various chemical processes, and electricity became more widely available to produce new goods or new, improved versions of old goods. Petroleum and hydroelectricity became major sources of power. During this time, the Industrial Revolution spread out of Western Europe and into the US and Japan.

Political, social and economic side effects
The Industrial Revolution led to widespread education, a wider franchise, and the development of mass communication in the political arena. Economically, conflicts arose between companies and their employees, as struggles for fair treatment and fair wages increased. Unions gained power and became more active. Government regulation over industries increased, but at the same time, growing businesses fought for the right to free enterprise. In the social sphere, populations increased and began to concentrate around centers of industry. Cities became larger and more densely populated. Scientific advancements led to more efficient agriculture, greater supply of goods, and increased knowledge of medicine and sanitation, leading to better overall health.

Nationalism in the eighteenth and nineteenth centuries

Nationalism, put simply, is a strong belief in, identification with, and allegiance to a particular nation and people. Nationalistic belief unified various areas that had previously seen themselves as fragmented, which led to patriotism and, in some cases, imperialism. As nationalism grew, individual nations sought to grow, bringing in other, smaller states that shared similar characteristics such as language and cultural beliefs. Unfortunately, a major side effect of these growing nationalistic beliefs was often conflict and outright war.

In Europe, imperialism led countries to spread their influence into Africa and Asia. Africa was eventually divided among several European countries that wanted the raw materials. Asia also came under European control, with the exception of China, Japan and Siam (now Thailand). In the US, Manifest Destiny became the rallying cry as the country expanded west. Italy and Germany formed larger nations from a variety of smaller states.

> **Review Video:** Nationalism
> *Visit **mometrix.com/academy** and enter **Code: 276165***

World War I

Europe
WWI began in 1914 with the assassination of Archduke Franz Ferdinand, heir to the throne of Austria-Hungary, by a Serbian national. This led to a conflict between Austria-Hungary and Serbia that quickly escalated into the First World War. Europe split into the Allies—Britain, France, and Russia, and later Italy, Japan, and the US, against the Central Powers—Austria-Hungary, Germany, the Ottoman Empire, and Bulgaria. As the war spread, countries beyond Europe became involved. The war left Europe deeply in debt, and particularly devastated the German economy. The ensuing Great Depression made matters worse, and economic devastation opened the door for communist, fascist, and socialist governments to gain power.

Trench warfare
Fighting during WWI largely took place in a series of trenches built along the Eastern and Western Fronts. These trenches added up to more than 24,000 miles. This produced fronts that stretched over 400 miles, from the coast of Belgium to the border of Switzerland. The Allies made use of straightforward open-air trenches with a front line, supporting lines, and communications lines. By contrast, the German trenches sometimes included well-equipped underground living quarters.

> **Review Video:** World War I
> *Visit **mometrix.com/academy** and enter **Code: 365382***

Communism and Socialism

At their roots, socialism and communism both focus on public ownership and distribution of goods and services. However, communism works toward revolution by drawing on what it sees to be inevitable class antagonism, eventually overthrowing the upper classes and the systems of capitalism. Socialism makes use of democratic procedures, building on the existing order. This was particularly true of the utopian socialists, who saw industrial capitalism as oppressive, not allowing workers to prosper.

While socialism struggled between the World Wars, communism took hold, especially in Eastern Europe. After WWII, democratic socialism became more common. Later, capitalism took a stronger hold again, and today most industrialized countries in the western world function under an economy that mixes elements of capitalism and socialism.

> ➢ **Review Video:** Socialism
> *Visit **mometrix.com/academy** and enter **Code**: **814221***

Rise of the Nazi party

The Great Depression had a particularly devastating effect on Germany's economy, especially after the US was no longer able to supply reconstruction loans to help the country regain its footing. With unemployment rising rapidly, dissatisfaction with the government grew. Fascist and Communist parties rose, promising change and improvement.

Led by Adolf Hitler, the fascist Nazi Party eventually gained power in Parliament based on these promises and the votes of desperate German workers. When Hitler became Chancellor, he launched numerous expansionist policies, violating the peace treaties that had ended WWI. His military buildup and conquering of neighboring countries sparked the aggression that soon led to WWII.

Blitzkrieg

The blitzkrieg, or "lightning war," consisted of fast, powerful surprise attacks that disrupted communications, made it difficult if not impossible for the victims to retaliate, and demoralized Germany's foes. The "blitz," or the aerial bombing of England in 1940, was one example, with bombings occurring in London and other cities 57 nights in a row. The Battle of Britain in 1940 also brought intense raids by Germany's air force, the Luftwaffe, mostly targeting ports and British air force bases. Eventually, Britain's Royal Air Force blocked the Luftwaffe, ending Germany's hopes for conquering Britain.

Battle of the Bulge

Following the D-Day Invasion, Allied forces gained considerable ground and began a major campaign to push through Europe. In December of 1944, Hitler launched a counteroffensive, attempting to retake Antwerp, an important port. The ensuing battle became the largest land battle on the war's Western Front, and was known as the Battle of the Ardennes, or the Battle of the Bulge. The battle lasted from December 16, 1944 to January 25, 1945. The Germans pushed forward, making inroads into Allied lines, but in the end the Allies brought the advance to a halt. The Germans were pushed back, with massive losses on both sides. However, those losses proved crippling to the German army.

Holocaust

As Germany sank deeper and deeper into dire economic straits, the tendency was to look for a person or group of people to blame for the problems of the country. With distrust of the Jewish people already ingrained, it was easy for German authorities to set up the Jews as scapegoats for Germany's problems. Under the rule of Hitler and the Nazi party, the "Final Solution" for the supposed Jewish problem was devised. Millions of Jews, as well as Gypsies, homosexuals, communists, Catholics, the mentally ill and others, simply named as criminals, were transported to concentration camps during the course of the war. At least six million were slaughtered in death camps such as Auschwitz, where horrible conditions and torture of prisoners were commonplace. The Allies were aware of rumors of mass slaughter throughout the war, but many discounted the reports. Only when troops went in to liberate the prisoners was the true horror of the concentration camps brought to light. The Holocaust resulted in massive loss of human life, but also in the loss and destruction of cultures. Because the genocide focused on specific ethnic groups, many traditions, histories, knowledge, and other cultural elements were lost, particularly among the Jewish and Gypsy populations. After World War II, the United Nations recognized genocide as a "crime against humanity." The UN passed the Universal Declaration of Human Rights in 1948 in order to further specify what rights the organization protected. Nazi war criminals faced justice during the Nuremberg Trials. There individuals, rather than their governments, were held accountable for war crimes.

> ➤ **Review Video:** The Holocaust
> *Visit **mometrix.com/academy** and enter **Code**: 219441*

Cold War

With millions of military and civilian deaths and over 12 million persons displaced, WWII left large regions of Europe and Asia in disarray. Communist governments moved in with promises of renewed prosperity and economic stability. The Soviet Union backed communist regimes in much of Eastern Europe. In China, Mao Zedong led communist forces in the overthrow of the Chinese Nationalist Party and instituted a communist government in 1949. While the new communist governments restored a measure of stability to much of Eastern Europe, it brought its own problems, with dictatorial governments and an oppressive police force. The spread of communism also led to several years of tension between communist countries and the democratic west, as the west fought to slow the spread of oppressive regimes throughout the world. With both sides in possession of nuclear weapons, tensions rose. Each side feared the other would resort to nuclear attack. This standoff lasted until 1989, when the Berlin Wall fell. The Soviet Union was dissolved two years later.

United Nations

The United Nations (UN) came into being toward the end of World War II. A successor to the less-than-successful League of Nations formed after World War I, the UN built and improved on those ideas. Since its inception, the UN has worked to bring the countries of the world together for diplomatic solutions to international problems, including sanctions and other restrictions. It has also initiated military action, calling for peacekeeping troops from member countries to move against countries violating UN policies. The Korean War was the first example of UN involvement in an international conflict.

Decolonization

A rise of nationalism among European colonies led to many of them declaring independence. India and Pakistan became independent of Britain in 1947, and numerous African and Asian colonies declared independence as well. This period of decolonization lasted into the 1960s. Some colonies moved successfully into independence but many, especially in Africa and Asia, struggled to create stable governments and economies, and suffered from ethnic and religious conflicts, some of which continue today.

Korean War

In 1910, Japan annexed Korea and maintained this control until 1945. After WWII, Soviet and US troops occupied Korea, with the Soviet Union controlling North Korea and the US controlling South Korea. In 1947, the UN ordered elections in Korea to unify the country but the Soviet Union refused to allow them to take place in North Korea, instead setting up a communist government. In 1950, the US withdrew troops, and the North Korean troops moved to invade South Korea. The Korean War was the first war in which the UN—or any international organization—played a major role. The US, Australia, Canada, France, Netherlands, Great Britain, Turkey, China, USSR and other countries sent troops at various times, for both sides, throughout the war. In 1953, the war ended in a truce, but no peace agreement was ever achieved, and Korea remains divided.

Vietnam War and involvement of France

Vietnam had previously been part of a French colony called French Indochina. The Vietnam War began with the First Indochina War from 1946-1954, in which France battled with the Democratic Republic of Vietnam, ruled by Ho Chi Minh.

In 1954, a siege at Dien Bien Phu ended in a Vietnamese victory. Vietnam was then divided into North and South, much like Korea. Communist forces controlled the North and the South was controlled by South Vietnamese forces, supported by the US. Conflict ensued, leading to another war. US troops eventually led the fight, in support of South Vietnam. The war became a major political issue in the US, with many citizens protesting American involvement. In 1975, South Vietnam surrendered, and Vietnam became the Socialist Republic of Vietnam.

Globalism

In the modern era, globalism has emerged as a popular political ideology. Globalism is based in the idea that all people and all nations are interdependent. Each nation is dependent on one or more other nations for production of and markets for goods, and for income generation. Today's ease of international travel and communication, including technological advances such as the airplane, has heightened this sense of interdependence. The global economy, and the general idea of globalism, has shaped many economic and political choices since the beginning of the twentieth century. Many of today's issues, including environmental awareness, economic struggles, and continued warfare, often require the cooperation of many countries if they are to be dealt with effectively.

Effects of globalization

Countries worldwide often seek the same resources, leading to high demand, particularly for nonrenewable resources. This can result in heavy fluctuations in price. One major example is the demand for petroleum products such as oil and natural gas. Increased travel and communication make it possible to deal with diseases in remote locations; however, this also allows diseases to be spread via travelers.

A major factor contributing to increased globalization over the past few decades has been the Internet. By allowing instantaneous communication with anyone nearly anywhere on the globe, the Internet has led to interaction between far-flung individuals and countries, and an ever increasing awareness of events all over the world.

Middle East in international relations and economics

The location on the globe, with ease of access to Europe and Asia, and its preponderance of oil deposits, makes the Middle Eastern countries crucial in many international issues, both diplomatic and economic. Because of its central location, the Middle East has been a hotbed for violence since before the beginning of recorded history. Conflicts over land, resources, and religious and political power continue in the area today, spurred by conflict over control of the area's vast oil fields as well as over territories that have been disputed for thousands of years.

> ➤ **Review Video:** Globalization: The Middle East
> *Visit **mometrix.com/academy** and enter **Code**: **655231***

Genocide

The three major occurrences of genocide in modern history other than the Holocaust are:
- Armenian genocide—from 1914 to 1918, the Young Turks, heirs to the Ottoman Empire, slaughtered between 800,000 and 1.5 million Armenians. This constituted approximately half of the Armenian population at the time.
- Russian purges under Stalin—scholars have attributed deaths between 3 and 60 million, both directly and indirectly, to the policies and edicts of Joseph Stalin's regime. The deaths took place from 1921 to 1953, when Stalin died. In recent years, many scholars have settled on a number of deaths near 20 million but this is still disputed today.
- Rwandan genocide—in 1994, hundreds of thousands of Tutsi, as well as Hutu who sympathized with them, were slaughtered during the Rwandan Civil War. The UN did not act or authorize intervention during these atrocities.

Government/Civics/Political Science

Political science

Political science focuses on studying different governments and how they compare to each other, general political theory, ways political theory is put into action, how nations and governments interact with each other, and a general study of governmental structure and function. Other elements of political science include the study of elections, governmental administration at various levels, development and action of political parties, and how values such as freedom, power, justice and equality are expressed in different political cultures. Political science also encompasses elements of other disciplines, including:

- History—how historical events have shaped political thought and process
- Sociology—the effects of various stages of social development on the growth and development of government and politics
- Anthropology—the effects of governmental process on the culture of an individual group and its relationships with other groups
- Economics—how government policies regulate distribution of products and how they can control and/or influence the economy in general

Government

Based on general political theory, the four major purposes of any given government are:

- Ensuring national security—the government protects against international, domestic and terrorist attacks and also ensures ongoing security through negotiating and establishing relationships with other governments.
- Providing public services—the government should "promote the general welfare," as stated in the Preamble to the US Constitution, by providing whatever is needed to its citizens.
- Ensuring social order—the government supplies means of settling conflicts among citizens as well as making laws to govern the nation, state, or city.
- Making decisions regarding the economy—laws help form the economic policy of the country, regarding both domestic and international trade and related issues. The government also has the ability to distribute goods and wealth to some extent among its citizens.

Origin of the state

There are four main theories regarding the origin of the state:

- Evolutionary—the state evolved from the family, with the head of state the equivalent of the family's patriarch or matriarch.
- Force—one person or group of people brought everyone in an area under their control, forming the first government.
- Divine Right—certain people were chosen by the prevailing deity to be the rulers of the nation, which is itself created by the deity or deities.
- Social Contract—there is no natural order. The people allow themselves to be governed to maintain social order, while the state in turn promises to protect the people they govern. If the government fails to protect its people, the people have the right to seek new leaders.

Influences of philosophers on political study

Ancient Greek philosophers Aristotle and Plato believed political science would lead to order in political matters, and that this scientifically organized order would create stable, just societies.

Thomas Aquinas adapted the ideas of Aristotle to a Christian perspective. His ideas stated that individuals should have certain rights, but also certain duties, and that these rights and duties should determine the type and extent of government rule. In stating that laws should limit the role of government, he laid the groundwork for ideas that would eventually become modern constitutionalism.

Niccolò Machiavelli, author of *The Prince*, was a proponent of politics based on power. He is often considered the founder of modern political science.

Thomas Hobbes, author of *Leviathan* (1651), believed that individual's lives were focused solely on a quest for power, and that the state must work to control this urge. Hobbes felt that people were completely unable to live harmoniously without the intervention of a powerful, undivided government.

John Locke published *Two Treatises of Government* in 1689. This work argued against the ideas of Thomas Hobbes. He put forth the theory of *tabula rasa*—that people are born with minds like blank slates. Individual minds are molded by experience, not innate knowledge or intuition. He also believed that all men should be independent and equal. Many of Locke's ideas found their way into the Constitution of the United States.

The two French philosophers, Montesquieu and Rousseau, heavily influenced the French Revolution (1789-1799). They believed government policies and ideas should change to alleviate existing problems, an idea referred to as "liberalism." Rousseau in particular directly influenced the Revolution with writings such as *The Social Contract* (1762) and *Declaration of the Rights of Man and of the Citizen* (1789). Other ideas Rousseau and Montesquieu espoused included:
- Individual freedom and community welfare are of equal importance
- Man's innate goodness leads to natural harmony
- Reason develops with the rise of civilized society
- Individual citizens carry certain obligations to the existing government

David Hume and Jeremy Bentham believed politics should have as its main goal maintaining "the greatest happiness for the greatest number." Hume also believed in empiricism, or that ideas should not be believed until the proof has been observed. He was a natural skeptic and always sought out the truth of matters rather than believing what he was told.

John Stuart Mill, a British philosopher as well as an economist, believed in progressive policies such as women's suffrage, emancipation, and the development of labor unions and farming cooperatives.

Johann Fichte and Georg Hegel, German philosophers in the late eighteenth and early nineteenth centuries, supported a form of liberalism grounded largely in socialism and a sense of nationalism.

Political orientations

The four main political orientations are:
- Liberal—liberals believe that government should work to increase equality, even at the expense of some freedoms. Government should assist those in need. Focus on enforced social justice and free basic services for everyone.
- Conservative—a conservative believes that government should be limited in most cases. The government should allow its citizens to help one another and solve their own problems rather than enforcing solutions. Business should not be overregulated, allowing a free market.
- Moderate—this ideology incorporates some liberal and some conservative values, generally falling somewhere between in overall belief.
- Libertarian—libertarians believe that the government's role should be limited to protecting the life and liberty of citizens. Government should not be involved in any citizen's life unless that citizen is encroaching upon the rights of another.

Principles of government

The six major principles of government as outlined in the United States Constitution are:
- Federalism—the power of the government does not belong entirely to the national government, but is divided between federal and state governments.
- Popular sovereignty—the government is determined by the people, and gains its authority and power from the people.
- Separation of powers—the government is divided into three branches, executive, legislative, and judicial, with each branch having its own set of powers.
- Judicial review—courts at all levels of government can declare laws invalid if they contradict the constitutions of individual states, or the US Constitution, with the Supreme Court serving as the final judicial authority on decisions of this kind.
- Checks and balances—no single branch can act without input from another, and each branch has the power to "check" any other, as well as balance other branches' powers.
- Limited government—governmental powers are limited and certain individual rights are defined as inviolable by the government.

Powers delegated to the national government

The structure of the US government divides power between national and state governments. Powers delegated to the federal government by the Constitution are:
- Expressed powers—powers directly defined in the Constitution, including power to declare war, regulate commerce, make money, and collect taxes
- Implied powers—powers the national government must have in order to carry out the expressed powers
- Inherent powers—powers inherent to any government, not expressly defined in the Constitution

Some of these powers, such as collection and levying of taxes, are also granted to the individual state governments.

Federalism

The way federalism should be practiced has been the subject of debate since writing of the Constitution. There were—and still are—two main factions regarding this issue:
- States' rights—those favoring the states' rights position feel that the state governments should take the lead in performing local actions to manage various problems.
- Nationalist—those favoring a nationalist position feel the national government should take the lead to deal with those same matters.

The flexibility of the Constitution has allowed the US government to shift and adapt as the needs of the country have changed. Power has often shifted from the state governments to the national government and back again, and both levels of government have developed various ways to influence each other.

Federalism has three major effects on public policy in the US:
- Determining whether the local, state, or national government originates policy
- Affecting how policies are made
- Ensuring policy-making functions under a set of limitations

Federalism also influences the political balance of power in the US by:
- making it difficult, if not impossible, for a single political party to seize total power
- ensuring that individuals can participate in the political system at various levels
- making it possible for individuals working within the system to be able to affect policy at some level, whether local or more widespread

Branches of the US government

The following are the three branches of the US Federal government and the individuals that belong to each branch:
- Legislative Branch—this consists of the two Houses of Congress: the House of Representatives and the Senate. All members of the Legislative Branch are elected officials.
- Executive Branch—this branch is made up of the President, Vice President, presidential advisors, and other various cabinet members. Advisors and cabinet are appointed by the President, but must be approved by Congress.
- Judicial Branch—the federal court system, headed by the Supreme Court.

The three branches of the Federal government each have specific roles and responsibilities:
- The Legislative Branch is largely concerned with law-making. All laws must be approved by Congress before they go into effect. They are also responsible for regulating money and trade, approving presidential appointments, and establishing organizations like the postal service and federal courts. Congress can also propose amendments to the Constitution, and can impeach, or bring charges against, the President. Only Congress can declare war.
- The Executive Branch carries out laws, treaties, and war declarations enacted by Congress. The President can also veto bills approved by Congress, and serves as commander-in-chief of the US military. The president appoints cabinet members, ambassadors to foreign countries, and federal judges.

- The Judicial Branch makes decisions on challenges as to whether laws passed by Congress meet the requirements of the US Constitution. The Supreme Court may also choose to review decisions made by lower courts to determine their constitutionality.

> ➤ **Review Video:** The Three Branches of the US Government
> *Visit* **mometrix.com/academy** *and enter* **Code**: **718704**

US citizenship

Anyone born in the US, born abroad to a US citizen, or who has gone through a process of naturalization is considered a citizen of the United States. It is possible to lose US citizenship as a result of conviction of certain crimes such as treason. Citizenship may also be lost if a citizen pledges an oath to another country or serves in the military of a country engaged in hostilities with the US. A US citizen can also choose to hold dual citizenship, work as an expatriate in another country without losing US citizenship, or even to renounce citizenship if he or she so chooses.

Citizens are granted certain rights under the US government. The most important of these are defined in the Bill of Rights, and include freedom of speech, religion, assembly, and a variety of other rights the government is not allowed to remove. A US citizen also has a number of duties:
- Paying taxes
- Loyalty to the government (though the US does not prosecute those who criticize or seek to change the government)
- Support and defense of the Constitution
- Serving in the Armed Forces when required by law
- Obeying laws as set forth by the various levels of government.

Responsibilities of a US citizen include:
- Voting in elections
- Respecting one another's rights and not infringing on them
- Staying informed about various political and national issues
- Respecting one another's beliefs

Bill of Rights

The first ten amendments of the US Constitution are known as the Bill of Rights. These amendments prevent the government from infringing upon certain freedoms that the founding fathers felt were natural rights that already belonged to all people. These rights included freedom of speech, freedom of religion, the right to bear arms, and freedom of assembly. Many of the rights were formulated in direct response to the way the colonists felt they had been mistreated by the British government.

The first ten amendments were passed by Congress in 1789. Three-fourths of the existing thirteen states had ratified them by December of 1791, making them official additions to the Constitution. The rights granted in the Bill of Rights are:

- First Amendment—freedom of religion, speech, freedom of the press, and the right to assemble and to petition the government
- Second Amendment—the right to bear arms
- Third Amendment—Congress cannot force individuals to house troops
- Fourth Amendment—protection from unreasonable search and seizure
- Fifth Amendment—no individual is required to testify against himself, and no individual may be tried twice for the same crime
- Sixth Amendment—right to criminal trial by jury, right to legal counsel
- Seventh Amendment—right to civil trial by jury
- Eighth Amendment—protection from excessive bail or cruel and unusual punishment
- Ninth Amendment—prevents rights not explicitly named in the Constitution from being taken away because they are not named
- Tenth Amendment—any rights not directly delegated to the national government, or not directly prohibited by the government from the states, belong to the states or to the people

In some cases, the government restricts certain elements of First Amendment rights. Some examples include:

- Freedom of religion—when a religion espouses illegal activities, the government often restricts these forms of religious expression. Examples include polygamy, animal sacrifice, and use of illicit drugs or illegal substances.
- Freedom of speech—this can be restricted if exercise of free speech endangers other people.
- Freedom of the press—laws prevent the press from publishing falsehoods.

In emergency situations such as wartime, stricter restrictions are sometimes placed on these rights, especially rights to free speech and assembly, and freedom of the press, in order to protect national security.

> **Review Video:** The Bill of Rights
> *Visit mometrix.com/academy and enter Code:* **585149**

Constitutional rights of criminals

The US Constitution makes allowances for the rights of criminals, or anyone who has transgressed established laws. There must be laws to protect citizens from criminals, but those accused of crimes must also be protected and their basic rights as individuals preserved. In addition, the Constitution protects individuals from the power of authorities to prevent police forces and other enforcement organizations from becoming oppressive. The fourth, fifth, sixth and eighth amendments specifically address these rights.

Equal protection under the law for all individuals

When the Founding Fathers wrote in the Declaration of Independence that "all men are created equal," they actually were referring to men, and in fact defined citizens as white men who owned land. However, as the country has developed and changed, the definition has expanded to more wholly include all people.

"Equality" does not mean all people are inherently the same, but it does mean they all should be granted the same rights and should be treated the same by the government. Amendments to the Constitution have granted citizenship and voting rights to all Americans regardless of race or gender. The Supreme Court evaluates various laws and court decisions to determine if they properly represent the idea of equal protection. One sample case was Brown v. Board of Education in 1954, which declared separate-but-equal treatment to be unconstitutional.

Civil liberty challenges addressed in current political discussions

The civil rights movements of the 1960s and ongoing struggle for the rights of women and other minorities have sparked challenges to existing law. In addition, debate has raged over how much information the government should be required to divulge to the public. Major issues in today's political climate include:
- Continued debate over women's rights, especially regarding equal pay for equal work
- Debate over affirmative action to encourage hiring of minorities
- Debate over civil rights of homosexuals, including marriage and military service
- Decisions as to whether minorities should be compensated for past discriminatory practices
- Balance between the public's right to know and the government's need to maintain national security
- Balance between the public's right to privacy and national security

Civil liberties and civil rights

While the terms "civil liberties" and "civil rights" are often used synonymously, in actuality their definitions are slightly different. The two concepts work together, however, to define the basics of a free state:
- "Civil liberties" defines the role of the state in providing equal rights and opportunities to individuals within that state. An example is non-discrimination policies with regards to granting citizenship.
- "Civil rights" defines the limitations of governmental rights, describing those rights that belong to individuals and which cannot be infringed upon by the government. Examples of these rights include freedom of religion, political freedom, and overall freedom to live as one chooses.

Suffrage and franchise

Suffrage and franchise both refer to the right to vote. As the US developed as a nation, there was much debate over which individuals should hold this right. In the early years, only white male landowners were granted suffrage. By the nineteenth century, most states had franchised, or granted the right to vote to, all adult white males. The Fifteenth Amendment of 1870 granted suffrage to former slave men. The Nineteenth Amendment gave women the right to vote in 1920, and in 1971 the Twenty-sixth Amendment expanded voting rights to include any US citizen over the age of eighteen. However, those who have not been granted full citizenship and citizens who have committed certain crimes do not have voting rights.

Changes in voting process

The first elections in the US were held by public ballot. However, election abuses soon became common, since public ballot made it easy to intimidate, threaten, or otherwise influence the votes of individuals or groups of individuals. New practices were put into play, including registering voters before elections took place, and using a secret or Australian ballot. In 1892, the introduction of the voting machine further privatized the voting process, since it allowed complete privacy for voting. Today debate continues about the accuracy of various voting methods, including high-tech voting machines and even low-tech punch cards.

Political parties

Different types and numbers of political parties can have a significant effect on how a government is run. If there is a single party, or a one-party system, the government is defined by that one party, and all policy is based on that party's beliefs. In a two-party system, two parties with different viewpoints compete for power and influence. The US is basically a two-party system, with checks and balances to make it difficult for one party to gain complete power over the other. There are also multi-party systems, with three or more parties. In multiparty systems, various parties will often come to agreements in order to form a majority and shift the balance of power.

George Washington was adamantly against the establishment of political parties, based on the abuses perpetrated by such parties in Britain. However, political parties developed in US politics almost from the beginning. Major parties throughout US history have included:
- Federalists and Democratic-Republicans—these parties formed in the late 1700s and disagreed on the balance of power between national and state government.
- Democrats and Whigs—these developed before the Civil War, based on disagreements about various issues such as slavery.
- Democrats and Republicans—the Republican Party developed after the Civil War, and the two parties debated issues centering on the treatment of the post-war South.

While third parties sometimes enter the picture in US politics, the government is basically a two-party system, dominated by the Democrats and Republicans.

> ➤ **Review Video:** Political Parties
> Visit *mometrix.com/academy* and enter *Code:* **640197**

Functions of political parties

Political parties form organizations at all levels of government. Activities of individual parties include:
- Recruiting and backing candidates for offices
- Discussing various issues with the public, increasing public awareness
- Working toward compromise on difficult issues
- Staffing government offices and providing administrative support

At the administrative level, parties work to ensure that viable candidates are available for elections and that offices and staff are in place to support candidates as they run for office and afterwards, when they are elected.

Process for choosing political candidate

Historically, in the quest for political office, a potential candidate has followed one of the following four processes:

- Nominating convention—an official meeting of the members of a party for the express purpose of nominating candidates for upcoming elections. The Democratic National Convention and the Republican National Convention, convened to announce candidates for presidency, are examples of this kind of gathering.
- Caucus—a meeting, usually attended by a party's leaders. Some states still use caucuses, but not all.
- Primary election—the most common method of choosing candidates today, the primary is a publicly held election to choose candidates.
- Petition—signatures are gathered to place a candidate on the ballot. Petitions can also be used to place legislation on a ballot.

Citizen participation in political process

In addition to voting for elected officials, American citizens are able to participate in the political process through several other avenues. These include:

- Participating in local government
- Participating in caucuses for large elections
- Volunteering to help political parties
- Running for election to local, state, or national offices

Individuals can also donate money to political causes, or support political groups that focus on specific causes such as abortion, wildlife conservation or women's rights. These groups often make use of representatives who lobby legislators to act in support of their efforts.

Campaign funding

Political campaigns are very expensive. In addition to the basic necessities of a campaign office, including office supplies, office space, etc., a large quantity of the money that funds a political campaign goes toward advertising. Money to fund a political campaign can come from several sources including:

- The candidate's personal funds
- Donations by individuals
- Special interest groups

The most significant source of campaign funding is special interest groups. Groups in favor of certain policies will donate money to candidates they believe will support those policies. Special interest groups also do their own advertising in support of candidates they endorse.

Free press and the media

The right to free speech guaranteed in the first amendment to the Constitution allows the media to report on government and political activities without fear of retribution. Because the media has access to information about the government, its policies and actions, as well as debates and discussions that occur in Congress, it can keep the public informed about the inner workings of the government. The media can also draw attention to injustices, imbalances of power, and other transgressions the government or government officials might commit. However, media outlets may, like special interest groups, align themselves with certain political viewpoints and skew their reports to fit that viewpoint. The rise of the Internet has made media reporting even more complex, as news can be found from an infinite variety of sources, both reliable and unreliable.

Anarchism, communism and dictatorship

Anarchists believe that all government should be eliminated and that individuals should rule themselves. Historically, anarchists have used violence and assassination to further their beliefs.

Communism is based on class conflict, revolution and a one-party state. Ideally, a communist government would involve a single government for the entire world. Communist government controls the production and flow of goods and services rather than leaving this to companies or individuals.

Dictatorship involves rule by a single individual. If rule is enforced by a small group, this is referred to as an oligarchy. Dictators tend to rule with a violent hand, using a highly repressive police force to ensure control over the populace.

Fascism and monarchy

Fascism centers on a single leader and is, ideologically, an oppositional belief to communism. Fascism includes a single party state and centralized control. The power of the fascist leader lies in the "cult of personality," and the fascist state often focuses on expansion and conquering of other nations. Monarchy was the major form of government for Europe through most of its history. A monarchy is led by a king or a queen. This position is hereditary, and the rulers are not elected. In modern times, constitutional monarchy has developed, where the king and queen still exist but most of the governmental decisions are made by democratic institutions such as a parliament.

Presidential system and socialism

A presidential system, like a parliamentary system, has a legislature and political parties, but there is no difference between the head of state and the head of government. Instead of separating these functions, an elected president performs both. Election of the president can be direct or indirect, and the president may not necessarily belong to the largest political party. In socialism, the state controls production of goods, though it does not necessarily own all means of production. The state also provides a variety of social services to citizens and helps guide the economy. A democratic form of government often exists in socialist countries.

Totalitarian and authoritarian systems of government

A totalitarian system believes everything should be under the control of the government, from resource production to the press to religion and other social institutions. All aspects of life under a totalitarian system must conform to the ideals of the government. Authoritarian governments practice widespread state authority, but do not necessarily dismantle all public institutions. If a church, for example, exists as an organization but poses no threat to the authority of the state, an authoritarian government might leave it as it is. While all totalitarian governments are by definition authoritarian, a government can be authoritarian without becoming totalitarian.

> **Review Video:** Authoritarian and Totalitarian Systems of Government
> *Visit mometrix.com/academy and enter Code:* **104046**

Parliamentary and democratic systems of government

In a parliamentary system, government involves a legislature and a variety of political parties. The head of government, usually a Prime Minister, is typically the head of the dominant party. A head of state can be elected, or this position can be taken by a monarch, as in Great Britain's constitutional monarchy system.

In a democratic system of government, the people elect their government representatives. The word "democracy" is a Greek term that means "rule of the people." There are two forms of democracy—direct and indirect. In a direct democracy, each issue or election is decided by a vote where each individual is counted separately. An indirect democracy employs a legislature that votes on issues that affect large numbers of people whom the legislative members represent. Democracy can exist as a parliamentary system or a presidential system. The US is a presidential, indirect democracy.

Realism, liberalism, institutionalism, and constructivism

The theory of realism states that nations are by nature aggressive, and work in their own self-interest. Relations between nations are determined by military and economic strength. The nation is seen as the highest authority. Liberalism believes states can cooperate, and that they act based on capability rather than power. This term was originally coined to describe Woodrow Wilson's theories on international cooperation. In institutionalism, institutions provide structure and incentive for cooperation among nations. Institutions are defined as a set of rules used to make international decisions. These institutions also help distribute power and determine how nations will interact. Constructivism, like liberalism, is based on international cooperation, but recognizes that perceptions countries have of each other can affect their relations.

> **Review Video:** Classical Liberalism
> *Visit mometrix.com/academy and enter Code:* **535938**

Foreign policy

Foreign policy is a set of goals, policies and strategies that determine how an individual nation will interact with other countries. These strategies shift, sometimes quickly and drastically, according to actions or changes occurring in the other countries. However, a nation's foreign policy is often based on a certain set of ideals and national needs.

Examples of US foreign policy include isolationism versus internationalism. In the 1800s, the US leaned more toward isolationism, exhibiting a reluctance to become involved in foreign affairs. The World Wars led to a period of internationalism, as the US entered these wars in support of other countries and joined the United Nations. Today's foreign policy tends more toward interdependence, or globalism, recognizing the widespread affects of issues like economic health. US foreign policy is largely determined by Congress and the president, influenced by the secretary of state, secretary of defense, and the national security adviser. Executive officials carry out policies. The main departments in charge of these day-to-day issues are the US Department of State, also referred to as the State Department. The Department of State carries out policy, negotiates treaties, maintains diplomatic relations, assists citizens traveling in foreign countries, and ensures that the president is properly informed of any international issues. The Department of Defense, the largest executive department in the US, supervises the armed forces and provides assistance to the President in his role as Commander-in-chief.

International organizations

Two types of international organizations are:
- Intergovernmental organizations (IGOs). These organizations are made up of members from various national governments. The UN is an example of an intergovernmental organization. Treaties among the member nations determine the functions and powers of these groups.
- Nongovernmental organizations (NGOs). An NGO lies outside the scope of any government and is usually supported through private donations. An example of an NGO is the International Red Cross, which works with governments all over the world when their countries are in crisis, but is formally affiliated with no particular country or government.

Diplomats

Diplomats are individuals who reside in foreign countries in order to maintain communications between that country and their home country. They help negotiate trade agreements and environmental policies, as well as conveying official information to foreign governments. They also help to resolve conflicts between the countries, often working to sort out issues without making the conflicts official in any way. Diplomats, or ambassadors, are appointed in the US by the president. Appointments must be approved by Congress.

UN

The United Nations (UN) helps form international policies by hosting representatives of various countries who then provide input into policy decisions. Countries who are members of the UN must agree to abide by all final UN resolutions, but this is not always the case in practice, as dissent is not uncommon. If countries do not follow UN resolutions, the UN can decide on sanctions against those countries, often economic sanctions, such as trade restriction. The UN can also send military forces to problem areas, with "peace keeping" troops brought in from member nations. An example of this function is the Korean War, the first war in which an international organization played a major role.

Geography

Geography

Geography literally means the study of the earth. Geographers study physical characteristics of the earth as well as man-made borders and boundaries. They also study the distribution of life on the planet, such as where certain species of animals can be found or how different forms of life interact. Major elements of the study of geography include:
- Locations
- Regional characteristics
- Spatial relations
- Natural and manmade forces that change elements of the earth

These elements are studied from regional, topical, physical and human perspectives. Geography also focuses on the origins of the earth as well as the history and backgrounds of different human populations.

<u>Physical and cultural geography</u>
Physical geography is the study of the physical characteristics of the earth: how they relate to each other, how they were formed, and how they develop. These characteristics include climate, land, and water, and also how they affect human population in various areas. Different landforms in combination with various climates and other conditions determine characteristics of various cultures.

Cultural geography is the study of how the various aspects of physical geography affect individual cultures. Cultural geography also compares various cultures: how their lifestyles and customs are affected by their geographical location, climate, and other factors, and how they interact with their environment.

Divisions of geographical study

The four divisions of geographical study and tools used are:
- Topical—the study of a single feature of the earth or one specific human activity that occurs world-wide.
- Physical—the various physical features of the earth, how they are created, the forces that change them, and how they are related to each other and to various human activities.
- Regional—specific characteristics of individual places and regions.
- Human—how human activity affects the environment. This includes study of political, historical, social, and cultural activities.

Tools used in geographical study include special research methods like mapping, field studies, statistics, interviews, mathematics, and use of various scientific instruments.

Ancient geographers

The following are three important ancient geographers and their contributions to the study of geography:
- Eratosthenes lived in ancient Greek times, and mathematically calculated the circumference of the earth and the tilt of the earth's axis. He also created the first map of the world.
- Strabo wrote a description of the ancient world called *Geographica* in seventeen volumes.
- Ptolemy, primarily an astronomer, was also an experienced mapmaker. He wrote a treatise entitled *Geography*, which was used by Christopher Columbus in his travels.

Analysis of areas of human population

In cities, towns, or other areas where many people have settled, geographers focus on distribution of populations, neighborhoods, industrial areas, transportation, and other elements important to the society in question. For example, they would map out the locations of hospitals, airports, factories, police stations, schools, and housing groups. They would also make note of how these facilities are distributed in relation to the areas of habitation, such as the number of schools in a certain neighborhood, or how many grocery stores are located in a specific suburban area. Another area of study and discussion is the distribution of towns themselves, from widely spaced rural towns to large cities that merge into each other to form a megalopolis.

Cartographers and maps

A cartographer is a mapmaker. Mapmakers produce detailed illustrations of geographic areas to record where various features are located within that area. These illustrations can be compiled into maps, charts, graphs, and even globes. When constructing maps, cartographers must take into account the problem of distortion. Because the earth is round, a flat map does not accurately represent the correct proportions, especially if a very large geographical area is being depicted. Maps must be designed in such a way as to minimize this distortion and maximize accuracy. Accurately representing the earth's features on a flat surface is achieved through projection.

Map projections

The three major types of projection used in creating world maps are:
- Cylindrical projection—this is created by wrapping the globe of the Earth in a cylindrical piece of paper, then using a light to project the globe onto the paper. The largest distortion occurs at the outermost edges.
- Conical projection—the paper is shaped like a cone and contacts the globe only at the cone's base. This type of projection is most useful for middle latitudes.
- Flat-Plane projections—also known as a Gnomonic projection, this type of map is projected onto a flat piece of paper that only touches the globe at a single point. Flat-plane projections make it possible to map out Great-Circle Routes, or the shortest route between one point and another on the globe, as a straight line.

Four specific types of map projections that are commonly used today are:

- Winkel tripel projection—this is the most common projection used for world maps, since it was accepted in 1998 by the National Geographic Society as a standard. The Winkel tripel projection balances size and shape, greatly reducing distortion.
- Robinson projection—east and west sections of the map are less distorted, but continental shapes are somewhat inaccurate.
- Goode homolosine projection—sizes and shapes are accurate, but distances are not. This projection basically represents a globe that has been cut into connected sections so that it can lie flat.
- Mercator projection—though distortion is high, particularly in areas farther from the equator, this cylindrical projection is commonly used by seafarers.

Map elements

The five major elements of any map are:

- Title—this tells basic information about the map, such as the area represented.
- Legend—also known as the key, the legend explains what symbols used on a particular map represent, such as symbols for major landmarks.
- Grid—this most commonly represents the Geographic Grid System, or latitude and longitude marks used to precisely locate specific locations.
- Directions—a compass rose or other symbol is used to indicate the cardinal directions.
- Scale—this shows the relation between a certain distance on the map and the actual distance. For example, one inch might represent one mile, or ten miles, or even more depending on the size of the map.

> ➤ **Review Video:** Elements of a Map
> *Visit **mometrix.com/academy** and enter **Code**: **437727***

Equal area map and conformal map

An equal area map is designed such that the proportional sizes of various areas are accurate. For example, if one land mass is one-fifth the size of another, the lines on the map will be shifted to accommodate for distortion so that the proportional size is accurate. In many maps, areas farther from the equator are greatly distorted; this type of map compensates for this phenomenon. A conformal map focuses on representing the correct shape of geographical areas, with less concern for comparative size.

Consistent scale map and thematic map

With a consistent scale map, the same scale, such as one inch=ten miles, is used throughout the entire map. This is most often used for maps of smaller areas, as maps that cover larger areas, such as the full globe, must make allowances for distortion. Maps of very large areas often make use of more than one scale, with scales closer to the center representing a larger area than those at the edges.

A thematic map is constructed to show very specific information about a chosen theme. For example, a thematic map might represent political information, such as how votes were distributed in an election, or could show population distribution or climatic features.

Relief map

A relief map is constructed to show details of various elevations across the area of the map. Higher elevations are represented by different colors than lower elevations. Relief maps often also show additional details, such as the overall ruggedness or smoothness of an area. Mountains would be represented as ridged and rugged, while deserts would be shown as smooth.

Elevation in relief maps can also be represented by contour lines, or lines that connect points of the same elevation. Some relief maps even feature textures, reconstructing details in a sort of miniature model.

Mountains, hills, plains, and valleys

- Mountains are elevated areas that measure 2,000 feet or more above sea level. Often steep and rugged, they usually occur in groups called chains or ranges. Six of the seven continents on Earth contain at least one range.
- Hills are of lower elevation than mountains, at about 500-2,000 feet. Hills are usually more rounded, and are found throughout every continent.
- Plains are large, flat areas and are usually very fertile. The majority of the Earth's population is supported by crops grown on vast plains.
- Valleys lie between hills and mountains. Depending on their location, their specific features can vary greatly, from fertile and habitable to rugged and inhospitable.

Plateaus, deserts, deltas, mesas, basins, foothills, marshes, and swamps

- Plateaus are elevated, but flat on top. Some plateaus are extremely dry, such as the Kenya Plateau, because surrounding mountains prevent them from receiving moisture.
- Deserts receive less than ten inches of rain per year. They are usually large areas, such as the Sahara Desert in Africa or the Australian Outback.
- Deltas occur at river mouths. Because the rivers carry sediment to the deltas, these areas are often very fertile.
- Mesas are flat, steep-sided mountains or hills. The term is sometimes used to refer to plateaus.
- Basins are areas of low elevation where rivers drain.
- Foothills are the transitional area between the plains and the mountains, usually consisting of hills that gradually increase in size as they approach the mountain range.
- Marshes and swamps are also lowlands, but they are very wet and largely covered in vegetation such as reeds and rushes.

Bodies of water

- Oceans are the largest bodies of water on Earth. They are salt water, and cover about two-thirds of the earth's surface. The four major oceans are the Atlantic, Pacific, Indian and Arctic.
- Seas are generally also salt water, but are smaller than oceans and surrounded by land. Examples include the Mediterranean Sea, the Caribbean Sea, and the Caspian Sea.
- Lakes are bodies of freshwater found inland. Sixty percent of all lakes are located in Canada.
- Rivers are moving bodies of water that flow from higher elevations to lower. They usually start as rivulets or streams, and grow until they finally empty into a sea or an ocean.
- Canals, such as the Panama Canal and the Suez Canal, are manmade waterways connecting two large bodies of water.

> ➤ **Review Video:** Bodies of Water
> *Visit **mometrix.com/academy** and enter **Code**:* **463122**

Communities

Communities, or groups of people who settle together in a specific area, typically gather where certain conditions exists. These conditions include:
- Easy access to resources such as food, water, and raw materials
- Ability to easily transport raw materials and goods, such as access to a waterway
- Room to house a sufficient work force

People also tend to form groups with others who are similar to them. In a typical community, people can be found who share values, a common language, and common or similar cultural characteristics and religious beliefs. These factors will determine the overall composition of a community as it develops.

Cities

Cities develop and grow as an area develops. Modern statistics show that over half of the world's people live in cities. That percentage is even higher in developed areas of the globe. Cities are currently growing more quickly in developing regions, and even established cities continue to experience growth throughout the world. In developing or developed areas, cities often are surrounded by a metropolitan area made up of both urban and suburban sections. In some places, cities have merged into each other and become a megalopolis—a single, huge city.

Cities develop differently in different areas of the world. The area available for cities to grow, as well as cultural and economic forces, drives how cities develop. For example, North American cities tend to cover wider areas. European cities tend to have better developed transportation systems. In Latin America, the richest inhabitants can be found in the city centers, while in North America wealthier inhabitants tend to live in suburban areas.

In other parts of the world, transportation and communication between cities is less developed. Recent technological innovations such as the cell phone have increased communication even in these areas. Urban areas must also maintain communication with rural areas in order to procure food, resources, and raw materials that cannot be produced within the city limits.

Weather and climate

Weather and climate are physical systems that affect geography. Though they deal with similar information, the way this information is measured and compiled is different. Weather involves daily conditions in the atmosphere that affect temperature, precipitation (rain, snow, hail, or sleet), wind speed, air pressure, and other factors. Weather focuses on the short-term—what the conditions will be today, tomorrow, or over the next few days.

In contrast, climate aggregates information about daily and seasonal weather conditions in a region over a long period of time. The climate takes into account average monthly and yearly temperatures, average precipitation over long periods of time, and the growing season of an area. Climates are classified according to latitude, or how close they lie to the earth's equator. The three major divisions are:
- Low Latitudes, lying from 0 to approximately 23.5 degrees latitude
- Middle Latitudes, found from approximately 23.5 to 66.5 degrees
- High Latitudes, found from approximately 66.5 degrees to the poles

Rainforests, savannas, and deserts occur in low latitudes:
- Rainforest climates, near the equator, experience high average temperatures and humidity, as well as relatively high rainfall.
- Savannas are found on either side of the rainforest region. Mostly grasslands, they typically experience dry winters and wet summers.
- Beyond the savannas lie the desert regions, with hot, dry climates, sparse rainfall, and temperature fluctuations of up to fifty degrees from day to night.

The climate regions found in the middle latitudes are:
- Mediterranean—the Mediterranean climate occurs between 30 and 40 degrees latitude, both north and south, on the western coasts of continents. Characteristics include a year-long growing season, hot, dry summers followed by mild winters, and sparse rainfall that occurs mostly during the winter months.
- Humid-subtropical—humid-subtropical regions are located on southeastern coastal areas. Winds that blow in over warm ocean currents produce long summers, mild winters, and a long growing season. These areas are highly productive, and support a larger part of the earth's population than any other climate.
- Humid-continental—the humid continental climate produces the familiar four seasons typical of a good portion of the US. Some of the most productive farmlands in the world lie in these climates. Winters are cold, summers are hot and humid.
- Marine—marine climates are found near water or on islands. Ocean winds help make these areas mild and rainy. Summers are cooler than humid-subtropical summers, but winters also bring milder temperatures due to the warmth of the ocean winds.
- Steppe—steppe climates, or prairie climates, are found far inland on large continents. Summers are hot and winters are cold, but rainfall is sparser than in continental climates.

- Desert—desert climates occur where steppe climates receive even less rainfall. Examples include the Gobi desert in Asia as well as desert areas of Australia and the southwestern US.

The high latitudes consist of two major climate areas, the tundra and taiga:
- Tundra means "marshy plain." Ground is frozen throughout long, cold winters, but there is little snowfall. During the short summers, it becomes wet and marshy. Tundras are not amenable to crops, but many plants and animals have adapted to the conditions.
- Taigas lie south of tundra regions, and include the largest forest areas in the world, as well as swamps and marshes. Large mineral deposits exist here, as well as many animals valued for their fur. In the winter, taiga regions are colder than the tundra, and summers are hotter. The growing season is short.

A vertical climate exists in high mountain ranges. Increasing elevation leads to varying temperatures, growing conditions, types of vegetation and animals, and occurrence of human habitation, often encompassing elements of various other climate regions.

> **Review Video:** <u>Weather and Climate</u>
> *Visit **mometrix.com/academy** and enter **Code**: **996776***

Factors that affect climate
Because the earth is tilted, its rotation brings about changes in seasons. Regions closer to the equator, and those nearest the poles, experience very little change in seasonal temperatures. Mid-range latitudes are most likely to experience distinct seasons. Large bodies of water also affect climate. Ocean currents and wind patterns can change the climate for an area that lies in typically cold latitude, such as England, to a much more temperate climate. Mountains can affect both short-term weather and long-term climates. Some deserts occur because precipitation is stopped by the wall of a mountain range.

Over time, established climate patterns can shift and change. While the issue is hotly debated, it has been theorized that human activity has also led to climate change.

Human systems

Human systems affect geography in the way in which they settle, form groups that grow into large-scale habitations, and even create permanent changes in the landscape. Geographers study movements of people, how they distribute goods among each other and to other settlements or cultures, and how ideas grow and spread. Migrations, wars, forced relocations, and trade can all spread cultural ideas, language, goods and other practices to wide-spread areas. Some major migrations or the conquering of one people by another have significantly changed cultures throughout history. In addition, human systems can lead to various conflicts or alliances to control access to and the use of natural resources.

North America
North America consists of 23 countries, including (in decreasing population order) the United States of America, Mexico, Canada, Guatemala, Cuba, Haiti, and the Dominican Republic. The US and Canada support similarly diverse cultures, as both were formed from groups of native races as well as large numbers of immigrants. Many North American cultures come from a mixture of indigenous and colonial European influences. Agriculture

- 85 -

is important to North American countries, while service industries and technology also play a large part in the economy. On average, North America supports a high standard of living and a high level of development and supports trade with countries throughout the world.

South America

Including Brazil (largest in area and population), Colombia, Argentina, Venezuela, Peru, and 10 more countries or territories, South America is largely defined by its prevailing languages. The majority of countries in South America speak Spanish or Portuguese. Most of South America has experienced a similar history, having been originally dominated by Native cultures, conquered by European nations. The countries of South America have since gained independence, but there is a wide disparity between various countries' economic and political factors. Most South American countries rely on only one or two exports, usually agricultural, with suitable lands often controlled by rich families. Most societies in South America feature major separations between classes, both economically and socially. Challenges faced by developing South American countries include geographical limitations, economic issues, and sustainable development, including the need to preserve the existing rainforests.

Europe

Europe contains a wide variety of cultures, ethnic groups, physical geographical features, climates, and resources, all of which have influenced the distribution of its varied population. Europe in general is industrialized and developed, with cultural differences giving each individual country its own unique characteristics. Greek and Roman influences played a major role in European culture, as did Christianity. European countries spread their beliefs and cultural elements throughout the world by means of migration and colonization. They have had a significant influence on nearly every other continent in the world. While Western Europe has been largely democratic, Eastern Europe functioned under communist rule for many years. The recent formation of the European Union (EU) has increased stability and positive diplomatic relations among European nations. Like other industrialized regions, Europe is now focusing on various environmental issues.

Russia

After numerous conflicts, Russia became a Communist state, known as the USSR. With the collapse of the USSR in 1991, the country has struggled in its transition to a market-driven economy. Attempts to build a workable system have led to the destruction of natural resources as well as problems with nuclear power, including accidents such as Chernobyl. To complete the transition to a market economy, Russia needs to improve its transportation and communication systems, and find a way to more efficiently use its natural resources.

The population of Russia is not distributed evenly, with three quarters of the population living west of the Ural Mountains. The people of Russia encompass over a hundred different ethnic groups. Over eighty percent of the population is ethnically Russian, and Russian is the official language of the country.

North Africa and Southwest and Central Asia

The largely desert climate of these areas has led most population centers to rise around sources of water, such as the Nile River. This area is the home of the earliest known civilizations and the origin of Christianity, Judaism, and Islam. After serving as the site of huge, independent civilizations in ancient times, North Africa and Southwest and Central Asia were largely parceled out as European colonies during the eighteenth and nineteenth centuries. The beginning of the twentieth century saw many of these countries gain their independence. Islam has served as a unifying force for large portions of these areas, and many of the inhabitants speak Arabic. In spite of the arid climate, agriculture is a large business, but the most valuable resource is oil. Centuries of conflict throughout this area have led to ongoing political problems. These political problems have also contributed to environmental issues.

Southern Africa

South of the Sahara Desert, Africa is divided into a number of culturally diverse nations. The inhabitants are unevenly distributed due to geographical limitations that prevent settlement in vast areas. AIDS has become a major plague throughout this part of Africa, killing millions, largely due to restrictive beliefs that prevent education about the disease, as well as abject poverty and unsettled political situations that make it impossible to manage the pandemic. The population of this area of Africa is widely diverse due to extensive migration. Many of the people still rely on subsistence farming for their welfare. Starvation and poverty are rampant due to drought and political instability. Some areas are far more stable than others due to greater availability of resources. These have been able to begin the process of industrialization.

South Asia

South Asia is home to one of the first human civilizations, which grew up in the Indus River Valley. With a great deal of disparity between rural and urban life, South Asia has much to do to improve the quality of life for its lower classes. Two major religions, Hinduism and Buddhism, have their origins in this region. Parts of South Asia, most notably India, were subject to British rule for several decades, and are still working to improve independent governments and social systems. Overall, South Asia is very culturally diverse, with a wide mix of religions and languages throughout. Many individuals are farmers, but a growing number have found prosperity in the spread of high-tech industries. Industrialization is growing in South Asia, but continues to face environmental, social, religious and economic challenges.

East Asia

Governments in East Asia are varied, ranging from communist to democratic governments, with some governments that mix both approaches. Isolationism throughout the area limited the countries' contact with other nations until the early twentieth century. The unevenly distributed population of East Asia consists of over one and a half billion people with widely diverse ethnic backgrounds, religions and languages. More residents live in urban areas than in rural areas, creating shortages of farm workers at times. Japan, Taiwan and South Korea are overall more urban, while China and Mongolia are more rural. Japan stands as the most industrial country of East Asia. Some areas of East Asia are suffering from major environmental issues. Japan has dealt with many of these problems and now has some of the strictest environmental laws in the world.
↳ Japan

Southeast Asia

Much of Southeast Asia was colonized by European countries during the eighteenth and nineteenth centuries, with the exception of Siam, now known as Thailand. All Southeast Asian countries are now independent, but the twentieth century saw numerous conflicts between communist and democratic forces.

Southeast Asia has been heavily influenced by both Buddhist and Muslim religions. Industrialization is growing, with the population moving in large numbers from rural to urban areas. Some have moved to avoid conflict, oppression, and poverty.

 Natural disasters, including volcanoes, typhoons, and flash flooding, are fairly common in Southeast Asia, creating extensive economic damage and societal disruption.

The South Pacific

South Pacific cultures originally migrated from Southeast Asia, creating hunter-gatherer or sometimes settled agricultural communities. European countries moved in during later centuries, seeking the plentiful natural resources of the area. Today, some South Pacific islands remain under the control of foreign governments, and culture in these areas mixes modern, industrialized society with indigenous culture. Population is unevenly distributed, largely due to the inhabitability of many parts of the South Pacific, such as the extremely hot desert areas of Australia. Agriculture still drives much of the economy, with tourism growing. Antarctica remains the only continent not claimed by a single country. There are no permanent human habitations in Antarctica, but scientists and explorers visit the area on a temporary basis.

Human-environment interaction

 Geography also studies the ways people interact with, use, and change their environment. The effects, reasons, and consequences of these changes are studied, as are the ways the environment limits or influences human behavior. This kind of study can help determine the best course of action when a nation or group of people are considering making changes to the environment, such as building a dam or removing natural landscape to build or expand roads. Study of the consequences can help determine if these actions are manageable and how long-term, detrimental results can be mitigated.

Physical geography and climate

North America

The largest amount of North America is the US and Canada, which have a similar distribution of geographical features, mountain ranges in both east and west, stretches of fertile plains through the center, and lakes and waterways. Both areas were shaped by glaciers, which also deposited highly fertile soil. Because they are so large, Canada and the US experience several varieties of climate, including continental climates with four seasons in median areas, tropical climates in the southern part of the US, and arctic climes in the far north. The remaining area of North America is comprised primarily of islands, including the Caribbean Isles and Greenland.

South America

South America contains a wide variety of geographical features including high mountains such as the Andes, wide plains, and high altitude plateaus. The region contains numerous natural resources, but many of them have remained unused due to various obstacles, including political issues, geographic barriers, and lack of sufficient economic power. Climate zones in South America are largely tropical, with rainforests and savannas, but vertical climate zones and grasslands also exist in places.

Europe

Europe spans a wide area with a variety of climate zones. In the east and south are mountain ranges, while the north is dominated by a plains region. The long coastline and the island nature of some countries, such as Britain, mean the climate is often warmer than other lands at similar latitudes, as the area is warmed by ocean currents. Many areas of western Europe have a moderate climate, while areas of the south are dominated by the classic Mediterranean climate. Europe carries a high level of natural resources. Numerous waterways help connect the inner regions with the coastal areas. Much of Europe is industrialized, and agriculture has been developed for thousands of years.

Russia

Russia's area encompasses part of Asia and Europe. From the standpoint of square footage alone, Russia is the largest country in the world. Due to its size, Russia encompasses a wide variety of climatic regions, including plains, plateaus, mountains, and tundra.

Russia's climate can be quite harsh, with rivers that are frozen most of the year, making transportation of the country's rich natural resources more difficult. Siberia, in northern Russia, is dominated by permafrost. Native peoples in this area still follow a hunting and gathering lifestyle, living in portable yurts and subsisting largely on herds of reindeer or caribou. Other areas include taiga with extensive, dense woods in north central Russia and more temperate steppes and grasslands in the southwest.

North Africa and Southwest and Central Asia

This area of the world is complex in its geographical structure and climate, incorporating seas, peninsulas, rivers, mountains, and numerous other features. Earthquakes are common, with tectonic plates in the area remaining active. Much of the world's oil lies in this area. The tendency of the large rivers of North Africa, especially the Nile, to follow a set pattern of drought and extreme fertility, led people to settle there from prehistoric times. As technology has advanced, people have tamed this river, making its activity more predictable and the land around it more productive. The extremely arid nature of many other parts of this area has also led to human intervention such as irrigation to increase agricultural production.

Southern Africa

South of the Sahara Desert, the high elevations and other geographical characteristics have made it very difficult for human travel or settlement to occur. The geography of the area is dominated by a series of plateaus. There are also mountain ranges and a large rift valley in the eastern part of the country. Contrasting the wide desert areas, Southern Africa contains numerous lakes, rivers, and world-famous waterfalls. The area has tropical climates, including rainforests, savannas, steppes, and desert areas. The main natural resources are minerals, including gems and water.

South Asia

The longest alluvial plain, a plain caused by shifting floodplains of major rivers and river systems over time, exists in South Asia. South Asia boasts three major river systems in the Ganges, Indus, and Brahmaputra. It also has large deposits of minerals, including iron ore that is in great demand internationally. South Asia holds mountains, plains, plateaus, and numerous islands. The climates range from tropical to highlands and desert areas. South Asia also experiences monsoon winds that cause a long rainy season. Variations in climate, elevation and human activity influence agricultural production.

East Asia

East Asia includes North and South Korea, Mongolia, China, Japan, and Taiwan. Mineral resources are plentiful but not evenly distributed throughout. The coastlines are long, and while the population is large, farmlands are sparse. As a result, the surrounding oceans have become a major source of sustenance. East Asia is large enough to also encompass several climate regions. Ocean currents provide milder climates to coastal areas, while monsoons provide the majority of the rainfall for the region. Typhoons are somewhat common, as are earthquakes, volcanoes and tsunamis. The latter occur because of the tectonic plates that meet beneath the continent and remain somewhat active.

Southeast Asia

Southeast Asia lies largely on the equator, and roughly half of the countries of the region are island nations. These countries include Indonesia, the Philippines, Vietnam, Thailand, Myanmar, and Malaysia (which is partially on the mainland and partially an island country). The island nations of Southeast Asia feature mountains that are considered part of the Ring of Fire an area where tectonic plates remain active, leading to extensive volcanic activity as well as earthquakes and tsunamis. Southeast Asia boasts many rivers as well as abundant natural resources, including gems, fossil fuels and minerals. There are basically two seasons—wet and dry. The wet season arrives with the monsoons. In general, Southeast Asia consists of tropical rainforest climates, but there are some mountain areas and tropical savannas.

Australia, Oceania and Antarctica

In the far southern hemisphere of the globe, Australia and Oceania present their own climatic combinations. Australia, the only island on earth that is also a continent, has extensive deserts as well as mountains and lowlands. The economy is driven by agriculture, including ranches and farms, and minerals. While the steppes bordering extremely arid inland areas are suitable for livestock, only the coastal areas receive sufficient rainfall for crops without using irrigation. Oceania refers to over 10,000 Pacific islands created by volcanic activity. Most of these have tropical climates with wet and dry seasons. New Zealand, Australia's nearest neighbor, boasts rich forests as well as mountain ranges and relatively moderate temperatures, including rainfall throughout the year. Antarctica is covered with ice. Its major resource consists of scientific information. It supports some wildlife, such as penguins, and little vegetation, mostly mosses or lichens.

Plate tectonics

According to the geological theory of plate tectonics, the earth's crust is made up of ten major and several minor tectonic plates. These plates are the solid areas of the crust. They float on top of the earth's mantle, which is made up of molten rock. Because the plates float on this liquid component of the earth's crust, they move, creating major changes in the earth's surface. These changes can happen very slowly over a long time period, such as in continental drift, or rapidly, such as when earthquakes occur. Interaction between the different continental plates can create mountain ranges, volcanic activity, major earthquakes, and deep rifts.

Subduction: when 1 cont. plate slides under another — leads to intense volcanic activity ⟹ Ring of Fire

Plate boundaries

Plate tectonics defines three types of plate boundaries, determined by the way in which the edges of the plates interact. These plate boundaries are:

- Convergent boundaries—the bordering plates move toward one another. When they collide directly, this is known as continental collision, which can create very large, high mountain ranges such as the Himalayas and the Andes. If one plate slides under the other, this is called subduction. Subduction can lead to intense volcanic activity. One example is the Ring of Fire that lies along the northern Pacific coastlines.
- Divergent boundaries—plates move away from each other. This movement leads to rifts such as the Mid-Atlantic Ridge and east Africa's Great Rift Valley.
- Transform boundaries—plate boundaries slide in opposite directions against each other. Intense pressure builds up along transform boundaries as the plates grind along each other's edges, leading to earthquakes. Many major fault lines, including the San Andreas Fault, lie along transform boundaries.

> ➤ **Review Video:** Plate Tectonics
> *Visit **mometrix.com/academy** and enter Code:* **623693**

Erosion, weathering, transportation and deposition

Erosion involves movement of any loose material on the earth's surface. This can include soil, sand, or rock fragments. These loose fragments can be displaced by natural forces such as wind, water, ice, plant cover, and human factors. Mechanical erosion occurs due to natural forces. Chemical erosion occurs as a result of human intervention and activities. Weathering occurs when atmospheric elements affect the earth's surface. Water, heat, ice, and pressure all lead to weathering. Transportation refers to loose material being moved by wind, water or ice. Glacial movement, for example, carries everything from pebbles to boulders, sometimes over long distances. Deposition is the result of transportation. When material is transported, it is eventually deposited, and builds up to create formations like moraines and sand dunes.

Effects of human interaction and conflict on geographical boundaries

Human societies and their interaction have led to divisions of territories into countries and various other subdivisions. While these divisions are at their root artificial, they are important to geographers in the discussion of interactions of various populations. Geographical divisions often occur through conflict between different human populations. The reasons behind these divisions include:

- Control of resources
- Control of important trade routes
- Control of populations

geo. div through conflict

Conflict often occurs due to religious, political, language, or race differences. Natural resources are finite and so often lead to conflict over how they are distributed among populations.

State sovereignty

State sovereignty recognizes the division of geographical areas into areas controlled by various governments or groups of people. These groups control not only the territory, but

- 91 -

also all its natural resources and the inhabitants of the area. The entire planet Earth is divided into political or administratively sovereign areas recognized to be controlled by a particular government with the exception of the continent of Antarctica.

Alliances

Alliances form between different countries based on similar interests, political goals, cultural values, or military issues. Six existing international alliances include:
- North Atlantic Treaty Organization (NATO)
- Common Market
- European Union (EU)
- United Nations (UN)
- Caribbean Community
- Council of Arab Economic Unity

In addition, very large companies and multi-national corporations can create alliances and various kinds of competition based on the need to control resources, production, and the overall marketplace.

Agricultural revolution

6 000 ya

The agricultural revolution began approximately six thousand years ago when the plow was invented in Mesopotamia. Using a plow drawn by animals, people were able to cultivate crops in large quantities rather than gathering available seeds and grains and planting them by hand. Because large-scale agriculture was labor intensive, this led to the development of stable communities where people gathered to make farming possible. As stable farming communities replaced groups of nomadic hunter-gatherers, human society underwent profound changes. Societies became dependent on limited numbers of crops as well as subject to the vagaries of weather. Trading livestock and surplus agricultural output led to the growth of large-scale commerce and trade routes.

Modification of surrounding environments by human populations

The agricultural revolution led human societies to begin changing their surroundings in order to accommodate their needs for shelter and room to cultivate food and to provide for domestic animals. Clearing ground for crops, redirecting waterways for irrigation purposes, and building permanent settlements all create major changes in the environment. Large-scale agriculture can lead to loose topsoil and damaging erosion. Building large cities leads to degraded air quality, water pollution from energy consumption, and many other side effects that can severely damage the environment. Recently, many countries have taken action by passing laws to reduce human impact on the environment and reduce the potentially damaging side effects. This is called environmental policy.

Ecology

Ecology is the study of the way living creatures interact with their environment. Biogeography explores the way physical features of the earth affect living creatures. Ecology bases its studies on three different levels of the environment:

- Ecosystem—this is a specific physical environment and all the organisms that live there.
- Biome—this is a group of ecosystems, usually consisting of a large area with similar flora and fauna as well as similar climate and soil. Examples of biomes include deserts, tropical rain forests, taigas, and tundra.
- Habitat—this is an area in which a specific species usually lives. The habitat includes the necessary soil, water, and resources for that particular species, as well as predators and other species that compete for the same resources.

Interactions between species

Different interactions occur among species and members of single species within a habitat. These interactions fall into three categories:

- Competition — competition occurs when different animals, either of the same species or of different species, compete for the same resources. Robins can compete with other robins for available food, but other insectivores also compete for these same resources.
- Predation— predation occurs when one species depends on the other species for food, such as a fox who subsists on small mammals.
- Symbiosis — symbiosis occurs when two different species exist in the same environment without negatively affecting each other. Some symbiotic relationships are beneficial to one or both organisms without harm occurring to either.

Ability to adapt

If a species is relocated from one habitat to another, it must adapt in order to survive. Some species are more capable of adapting than others. Those that cannot adapt will not survive. There are different ways a creature can adapt, including behavior modification as well as structure or physiological changes. Adaptation is also vital if an organism's environment changes around it. Although the creature has not been relocated, it finds itself in a new environment that requires changes in order to survive. The more readily an organism can adapt, the more likely it is to survive. The almost infinite ability of humans to adapt is a major reason why they are able to survive in almost any habitat in any area of the world.

Biodiversity

Biodiversity refers to the variety of habitats that exist on the planet, as well as the variety of organisms that can exist within these habitats. A greater level of biodiversity makes it more likely that an individual habitat will flourish along with the species that depend upon it. Changes in habitat, including climate change, human intervention, or other factors, can reduce biodiversity by causing the extinction of certain species.

Economics

Economics

Economics is the study of the ways specific societies allocate resources to individuals and groups within that society. Also important are the choices society makes regarding what efforts or initiatives are funded and which are not. Since resources in any society are finite, allocation becomes a vivid reflection of that society's values. In general, the economic system that drives an individual society is based on:

- What goods are produced
- How those goods are produced
- Who acquires the goods or benefits from them

Economics consists of two main categories: macroeconomics, which studies larger systems, and microeconomics, which studies smaller systems.

Market economy *vs. planned economy*

A market economy is based on supply and demand. Demand has to do with what customers want and need, as well as what quantity those consumers are able to purchase based on other economic factors. Supply refers to how much can be produced to meet demand, or how much suppliers are willing and able to sell. Where the needs of consumers meet the needs of suppliers is referred to as a market equilibrium price. This price varies depending on many factors, including the overall health of a society's economy, overall beliefs and considerations of individuals in society. The following is a list of terms defined in the context of a market economy:

- Elasticity—this is based on how the quantity of a particular product responds to the price demanded for that product. If quantity responds quickly to changes in price, the supply/demand for that product is said to be elastic. If it does not respond quickly, then the supply/demand is inelastic.
- Market efficiency—this occurs when a market is capable of producing output high enough to meet consumer demand, that market is efficient.
- Comparative advantage—in the field of international trade, this refers to a country focusing on a specific product that it can produce it more efficiently and more cheaply, or at a lower opportunity cost, than another country, thus giving it a comparative advantage in production.

> ➤ **Review Video:** Market Economy
> *Visit mometrix.com/academy and enter Code:* **460547**

Comparison to planned economy
In a market economy, supply and demand are determined by consumers. In a planned economy, a public entity or planning authority makes the decisions about what resources will be produced, how they will be produced, and who will be able to benefit from them. The means of production, such as factories, are also owned by a public entity rather than by private interests. In market socialism, the economic structure falls somewhere between the market economy and the planned economy. Planning authorities determine allocation of

- 94 -

resources at higher economic levels, while consumer goods are driven by a market economy.

Microeconomics

While economics generally studies how resources are allocated, microeconomics focuses on economic factors such as the way consumers behave, how income is distributed, and output and input markets. Studies are limited to the industry or firm level, rather than an entire country or society. Among the elements studied in microeconomics are factors of production, costs of production, and factor income. These factors determine production decisions of individual firms, based on resources and costs.

> ➤ **Review Video:** Microeconomics
> *Visit **mometrix.com/academy** and enter **Code**: **779207***

Classification of markets

The conditions prevailing in a given market are used to classify markets. Conditions considered include:
- Existence of competition
- Number and size of suppliers
- Influence of suppliers over price
- Variety of available products
- Ease of entering the market

Once these questions are answered, an economist can classify a certain market according to its structure and the nature of competition within the market.

Market failure

When any of the elements for a successfully competitive market are missing, this can lead to a market failure. Certain elements are necessary to create what economists call "perfect competition." If one of these factors is weak or lacking, the market is classified as having "imperfect competition." Worse than imperfect competition, though, is a market failure. There are five major types of market failure:
- Inadequate competition
- Inadequate information
- Immobile resources
- Negative externalities, or side effects
- Failure to provide public goods

Externalities are side effects of a market that affect third parties. These effects can be either negative or positive.

> ➤ **Review Video:** Market Failure
> *Visit **mometrix.com/academy** and enter **Code**: **198450***

Factors of production and costs of production

Every good and service requires certain resources, or inputs. These inputs are referred to as factors of production. Every good and service requires four factors of production:

- Labor
- Capital
- Land
- Entrepreneurship

These factors can be fixed or variable, and can produce fixed or variable costs. Examples of fixed costs include land and equipment. Variable costs include labor. The total of fixed and variable costs makes up the cost of production.

Factor income

Factors of production each have an associated factor income. Factors that earn income include:

- Labor—earns wages
- Capital—earns interest
- Land—earns rent
- Entrepreneurship—earns profit

Each factor's income is determined by its contribution. In a market economy, this income is not guaranteed to be equal. How scarce the factor is and the weight of its contribution to the overall production process determines the final factor income.

Output market

The four kinds of market structures in an output market are:

- Perfect competition—all existing firms sell an identical product. The firms are not able to control the final price. In addition, there is nothing that makes it difficult to become involved in or leave the industry. Anything that would prevent entering or leaving an industry is called a barrier to entry. An example of this market structure is agriculture.
- Monopoly—a single seller controls the product and its price. Barriers to entry, such as prohibitively high fixed cost structures, prevent other sellers from entering the market.
- Monopolistic competition—a number of firms sell similar products, but they are not identical, such as different brands of clothes or food. Barriers to entry are low.
- Oligopoly—only a few firms control the production and distribution of products, such as automobiles. Barriers to entry are high, preventing large numbers of firms from entering the market.

Barr

- 96 -

Monopolies

Four types of monopolies are:
- Natural monopoly—a single supplier has a distinct advantage over the others.
- Geographic monopoly—only one business offers the product in a certain area.
- Technological monopoly—a single company controls the technology necessary to supply the product.
- Government monopoly—a government agency is the only provider of a specific good or service.

Control by the US government

The US government has passed several acts to regulate businesses, including:
- Sherman Antitrust Act (1890)—this prohibited trusts, monopolies, and any other situations that eliminated competition.
- Clayton Antitrust Act (1914)—this prohibited price discrimination.
- Robinson-Patman Act (1936)—this strengthened provisions of the Clayton Antitrust Act, requiring businesses to offer the same pricing on products to any customer.

The government has also taken other actions to ensure competition, including requirements for public disclosure. The Securities and Exchange Commission (SEC) requires companies that provide public stock to provide financial reports on a regular basis. Because of the nature of their business, banks are further regulated and required to provide various information to the government.

Marketing and utility

Marketing consists of all of the activity necessary to convince consumers to acquire goods. One major way to move products into the hands of consumers is to convince them that any single product will satisfy a need. The ability of a product or service to satisfy the need of a consumer is called utility. There are four types of utility:
- Form utility—a product's desirability lies in its physical characteristics.
- Place utility—a product's desirability is connected to its location and convenience.
- Time utility—a product's desirability is determined by its availability at a certain time.
- Ownership utility—a product's desirability is increased because ownership of the product passes to the consumer.

Marketing behavior will stress any or all of these types of utility when marketing to the consumer.

Determining a product's market

Successful marketing depends not only on convincing customers they need the product, but also on focusing the marketing towards those who already have a need or desire for the product. Before releasing a product into the general marketplace, many producers will test markets to determine which will be the most receptive to the product.

There are three steps usually taken to evaluate a product's market:

- Market research—this involves researching a market to determine if it will be receptive to the product.
- Market surveys—a part of market research, market surveys ask consumers specific questions to help determine the marketability of a product to a specific group.
- Test marketing—this includes releasing the product into a small geographical area to see how it sells. Often test marketing is followed by wider marketing if the product does well.

Marketing plan

Once these elements have all been determined, the producer can proceed with production and distribution of his product.

- Product—this includes any elements pertaining directly to the product, such as packaging, presentation, or services to include along with it.
- Price—this calculates cost of production, distribution, advertising, etc., as well as the desired profit to determine the final price.
- Place—this determines which outlets will be used to sell the product, whether traditional outlets or through direct mail or Internet marketing.
- Promotion—this involves ways to let consumers know the product is available, through advertising and other means.

> **Review Video:** Marketing Plan
> *Visit **mometrix.com/academy** and enter **Code**: **983409**

Distribution channels

Distribution channels determine the route a product takes on its journey from producer to consumer, and can also influence the final price and availability of the product. There are two major forms of distributions: wholesale and retail. A wholesale distributor buys in large quantities and then resells smaller amounts to other businesses. Retailers sell directly to the consumers rather than to businesses. In the modern marketplace, additional distribution channels have grown up with the rise of markets such as club warehouse stores as well as purchasing through catalogs or over the Internet. Most of these newer distribution channels bring products more directly to the consumer, eliminating the need for middlemen.

Distribution of income and poverty

Distribution of income in any society ranges from poorest to richest. In most societies, income is not distributed evenly. To determine income distribution, family incomes are ranked from lowest to highest. These rankings are divided into five sections called quintiles, which are compared to each other. The uneven distribution of income is often linked to higher levels of education and ability in the upper classes, but can also be due to other factors such as discrimination and existing monopolies. The income gap in America continues to grow, largely due to growth in the service industry, changes in the American family unit and reduced influence of labor unions. Poverty is defined by comparing incomes to poverty guidelines. Poverty guidelines determine the level of income necessary for a family to function. Those below the poverty line are often eligible for assistance from government agencies.

Consumer behavior

The two major types of consumer behavior as defined in macroeconomics are:
- Marginal propensity to consume defines the tendency of consumers to increase spending in conjunction with increases in income. In general, individuals with greater income will buy more. As individuals increase their income through job changes or growth of experience, they will also increase spending.
- Utility is a term that describes the satisfaction experienced by a consumer in relation to acquiring and using a good or service. Providers of goods and services will stress utility to convince consumers they want the products being presented.

Macroeconomics

Macroeconomics examines economies on a much larger level than microeconomics. While microeconomics studies economics on a firm or industry level, macroeconomics looks at economic trends and structures on a national level. Variables studied in macroeconomics include:
- Output
- Consumption
- Investment
- Government spending
- Net exports

The overall economic condition of a nation is defined as the Gross Domestic Product, or GDP. GDP measures a nation's economic output over a limited time period, such as a year.

> **Review Video:** Microeconomics and Macroeconomics
> *Visit **mometrix.com/academy** and enter **Code**: **538837***

GDP

The two major ways to measure the Gross Domestic Product of a country are:
- The expenditures approach calculates the GDP based on how much money is spent in each individual sector.
- The income approach calculates the GDP based on how much money is earned in each sector.

Both methods yield the same results and both of these calculation methods are based on four economic sectors that make up a country's macro-economy:
- Consumers
- Business
- Government
- Foreign sector

Several factors must be considered in order to accurately calculate the GDP using the incomes approach. Income factors are:
- Wages paid to laborers, or Compensation of Employees
- Rental income derived from land
- Interest income derived from invested capital
- Entrepreneurial income

Entrepreneurial income consists of two forms. Proprietor's income is income that comes back to the entrepreneur himself. Corporate profit is income that goes back into the corporation as a whole. Corporate profit is divided by the corporation into corporate profits taxes, dividends, and retained earnings. Two other figures must be subtracted in the incomes approach. These are indirect business taxes, including property and sales taxes, and depreciation.

Effects of the population

Changes in population can affect the calculation of a nation's GDP, particularly since GDP and GNP (Gross National Product) are generally measured per capita. If a country's economic production is low, but the population is high, the income per individual will be lower than if the income is high and the population is lower. Also, if the population grows quickly and the income grows slowly, individual income will remain low or even drop drastically. Population growth can also affect overall economic growth. Economic growth requires both that consumers purchase goods and workers produce them. A population that does not grow quickly enough will not supply enough workers to support rapid economic growth.

Ideal balance in an economy and phases in national economies

Ideally, an economy functions efficiently, with the aggregate supply, or the amount of national output, equal to the aggregate demand, or the amount of the output that is purchased. In these cases, the economy is stable and prosperous. However, economies more typically go through phases. These phases are:
- Boom—GDP is high and the economy prospers
- Recession—GDP falls, unemployment rises
- Trough—the recession reaches its lowest point
- Recovery—unemployment lessens, prices rise, and the economy begins to stabilize again

These phases tend to repeat in cycles that are not necessarily predictable or regular.

Unemployment and inflation

When demand outstrips supply, prices are driven artificially high, or inflated. This occurs when too much spending causes an imbalance in the economy. In general, inflation occurs because an economy is growing too quickly. When there is too little spending and supply has moved far beyond demand, a surplus of product results. Companies cut back on production, reduce the number of employees, and unemployment rises as people lose their jobs. This imbalance occurs when an economy becomes sluggish. In general, both these economic instability situations are caused by an imbalance between supply and demand. Government intervention may be necessary to stabilize an economy when either inflation or unemployment becomes too serious.

<u>Forms of unemployment</u>
- Frictional—when workers change jobs and are unemployed while waiting for new jobs
- Structural—when economic shifts reduce the need for workers
- Cyclical—when natural business cycles bring about loss of jobs
- Seasonal—when seasonal cycles reduce the need for certain jobs
- Technological—when advances in technology result in elimination of certain jobs

Any of these factors can increase unemployment in certain sectors. Inflation is classified by the overall rate at which it occurs:
- Creeping inflation—this is an inflation rate of about 1-3% annually.
- Walking inflation—this is an inflation rate of 3-10% annually.
- Galloping inflation—this is a high inflation rate of more than 10% but less than 1000% annually.
- Hyperinflation—this is an inflation rate over 1000% per year. Hyperinflation usually leads to complete monetary collapse in a society, as individuals become unable to generate sufficient income to purchase necessary goods.

<u>Government intervention policies</u>
When an economy becomes too imbalanced, either due to excessive spending or not enough spending, government intervention often becomes necessary to put the economy back on track. Government Fiscal Policy can take several forms, including:
- Contractionary policy
- Expansionary policy
- Monetary policy

Contractionary policies help counteract inflation. These include increasing taxes and decreasing government spending to slow spending in the overall economy. Expansionary policies increase government spending and lower taxes in order to reduce unemployment and increase the level of spending in the economy overall. Monetary policy can take several forms, and affects the amount of funds available to banks for making loans.

Populations and population growth

Populations are studied by size, rates of growth due to immigration, the overall fertility rate, and life expectancy. For example, though the population of the United States is considerably larger than it was two hundred years ago, the rate of population growth has decreased greatly, from about three percent per year to less than one percent per year. In the US, the fertility rate is fairly low, with most choosing not to have large families, and life expectancy is high, creating a projected imbalance between older and younger people in the near future. In addition, immigration and the mixing of racially diverse cultures are projected to increase the percentages of Asians, Hispanics and African-Americans.

Money

Money is used in three major ways:
- As an accounting unit
- As a store of value
- As an exchange medium

In general, money must be acceptable throughout a society in exchange for debts or to purchase goods and services. Money should be relatively scarce, its value should remain stable, and it should be easily carried, durable, and easy to divide up. There are three basic types of money: commodity, representative and fiat. Commodity money includes gems or precious metals. Representative money can be exchanged for items such as gold or silver which have inherent value. Fiat money, or legal tender, has no inherent value but has been declared to function as money by the government. It is often backed by gold or silver, but not necessarily on a one-to-one ratio.

<u>US money</u>
Money in the US is not just currency. When economists calculate the amount of money available, they must take into account other factors such as deposits that have been placed in checking accounts, debit cards and "near moneys" such as savings accounts, that can be quickly converted into cash. Currency, checkable deposits and traveler's checks, referred to as M1, are added up, and then M2 is calculated by adding savings deposits, CDs and various other monetary deposits. The final result is the total quantity of available money.

Monetary policy and the Federal Reserve System

The Federal Reserve System, also known as the Fed, implements all monetary policy in the US. Monetary policy regulates the amount of money available in the American banking system. The Fed can decrease or increase the amount of available money for loans, thus helping regulate the national economy. Monetary policies implemented by the Fed are part of expansionary or contractionary monetary policies that help counteract inflation or unemployment. The discount rate is an interest rate charged by the Fed when banks borrow money from them. A lower discount rate leads banks to borrow more money, leading to increased spending. A higher discount rate has the opposite effect.

> **Review Video:** <u>Monetary Policy</u>
> *Visit **mometrix.com/academy** and enter **Code**: **662298***

Banks

Banks earn their income by loaning out money and charging interest on those loans. If less money is available, fewer loans can be made, which affects the amount of spending in the overall economy. While banks function by making loans, they are not allowed to loan out all the money they hold in deposit. The amount of money they must maintain in reserve is known as the reserve ratio. If the reserve ratio is raised, less money is available for loans and spending decreases. A lower reserve ratio increases available funds and increases spending. This ratio is determined by the Federal Reserve System.

Open Market Operations

The Federal Reserve System can also expand or contract the overall money supply through open market operations. In this case, the Fed can buy or sell bonds it has purchased from banks or individuals. When the Fed buys bonds, more money is put into circulation, creating an expansionary situation to stimulate the economy. When the Fed sells bonds, money is withdrawn from the system, creating a contractionary situation to slow an economy suffering from inflation. Because of international financial markets, however, American banks often borrow and lend money in markets outside the US. By shifting their attention to international markets, domestic banks and other businesses can circumvent whatever contractionary policies the Fed may have put into place.

International trade

International trade can take advantage of broader markets, bringing a wider variety of products within easy reach. By contrast, it can also allow individual countries to specialize in particular products that they can produce easily, such as those for which they have easy access to raw materials. Other products, more difficult to make domestically, can be acquired through trade with other nations. International trade requires efficient use of native resources as well as sufficient disposable income to purchase native and imported products. Many countries in the world engage extensively in international trade, but others still face major economic challenges.

Developing nations

The five major characteristics of a developing nation are:
- Low GDP
- Rapid growth of population
- Economy that depends on subsistence agriculture
- Poor conditions, including high infant mortality rates, high disease rates, poor sanitation, and insufficient housing
- Low literacy rate

Developing nations often function under oppressive governments that do not provide private property rights and withhold education and other rights from women. They also often feature an extreme disparity between upper and lower classes, with little opportunity for the lower classes to improve their position.

Stages of economic development
Economic development occurs in three stages that are defined by the activities that drive the economy:
- Agricultural stage
- Manufacturing stage
- Service sector stage

In developing countries, it is often difficult to acquire the necessary funding to provide equipment and training to move into the advanced stages of economic development. Some can receive help from developed countries via foreign aid and investment or international organizations such as the International Monetary Fund or the World Bank. Having developed countries provide monetary, technical, or military assistance can help developing countries move forward to the next stage in their development.

Obstacles to economic growth
Developing nations typically struggle to overcome obstacles that prevent or slow economic development. Major obstacles can include:
- Rapid, uncontrolled population growth
- Trade restrictions
- Misused resources, often perpetrated by the government
- Traditional beliefs that can slow or reject change

Corrupt, oppressive governments often hamper the economic growth of developing nations, creating huge economic disparities and making it impossible for individuals to advance, in turn preventing overall growth. Governments sometimes export currency, called capital flight, which is detrimental to a country's economic development. In general, countries are more likely to experience economic growth if their governments encourage entrepreneurship and provide private property rights.

Problems with rapid industrialization

Rapid growth throughout the world leaves some nations behind, and sometimes spurs their governments to move forward too quickly into industrialization and artificially rapid economic growth. While slow or nonexistent economic growth causes problems in a country, overly rapid industrialization carries its own issues. Four major problems encountered due to rapid industrialization are:
- Use of technology not suited to the products or services being supplied
- Poor investment of capital
- Lack of time for the population to adapt to new paradigms
- Lack of time to experience all stages of development and adjust to each stage

Economic failures in Indonesia were largely due to rapid growth that was poorly handled.

E-commerce

The growth of the Internet has brought many changes to our society, not the least of which is the modern way of business. Where supply channels used to move in certain necessary ways, many of these channels are now bypassed as e-commerce makes it possible for nearly any individual to set up a direct market to consumers, as well as direct interaction with suppliers. Competition is fierce. In many instances e-commerce can provide nearly instantaneous gratification, with a wide variety of products. Whoever provides the best product most quickly often rises to the top of a marketplace. How this added element to the marketplace will affect the economy in the future remains to be seen. Many industries are still struggling with the best ways to adapt to the rapid, continuous changes.

Knowledge economy

The knowledge economy is a growing sector in the economy of developed countries, and includes the trade and development of:
- Data
- Intellectual property
- Technology, especially in the area of communications

Knowledge as a resource is steadily becoming more and more important. What is now being called the Information Age may prove to bring about changes in life and culture as significant as those brought on by the Agricultural and Industrial Revolutions.

Cybernomics

Related to the knowledge economy is what has been dubbed "cybernomics," or economics driven by e-commerce and other computer-based markets and products. Marketing has changed drastically with the growth of cyber communication, allowing suppliers to connect one-on-one with their customers. Other issues coming to the fore regarding cybernomics include:

- Secure online trade
- Intellectual property rights
- Rights to privacy
- Bringing developing nations into the fold

As these issues are debated and new laws and policies developed, the face of many industries continues to undergo drastic change. Many of the old ways of doing business no longer work, leaving industries scrambling to function profitably within the new system.

Practice Test

Practice Questions

1. Which of the following is incorrect regarding the Virginia Companies?
   a. One of these companies, the Virginia Company of Plymouth, made its base in North America
   b. One of these companies, the Virginia Company of London, made its base in Massachusetts
   c. One company had a charter to colonize America between the Hudson and Cape Fear rivers
   d. One company had a charter to colonize America from the Potomac River to north Maine

2. Which of the following is not a correct statement regarding the Pilgrims?
   a. The Pilgrims left England in 1620 on the ship known as the Mayflower and landed at Cape Cod
   b. The Pilgrims were led by William Bradford with a charter from the London Company
   c. The Pilgrims were a group of Puritans who left England to escape religious persecution
   d. The Pilgrims were a group of separatists who migrated to leave the Church of England

3. Which of the following is not true regarding British mercantilism and the American colonies?
   a. English mercantilists held the belief that the government should regulate all economic enterprise
   b. The many crops produced on American colony farms contributed to English mercantilism
   c. The Navigation Acts were passed by Parliament between 1650 and 1700 to further mercantilism
   d. British mercantilism fueled wars with Holland, but did not contribute to American prosperity

4. Which of the following wars included no major army battles on American soil and no major changes in territories?
   a. Queen Anne's War
   b. King William's War
   c. King George's War
   d. The French and Indian War

5. Which of the following is true about the Enlightenment?
    a. The Enlightenment was a philosophical movement that began in America and spread to Europe
    b. One of the most central premises of the Enlightenment was the importance of God in the world
    c. John Locke believed that governments should not be deposed for violating social or political rights
    d. Of those who embraced the Enlightenment in America, the best known was Benjamin Franklin

6. Which of these factors was not a direct contributor to the beginning of the American Revolution?
    a. The attitudes of American colonists toward Great Britain following the French and Indian War
    b. The attitudes of leaders in Great Britain toward the American colonies and imperialism
    c. James Otis's court argument against Great Britain's Writs of Assistance as breaking natural law
    d. Lord Grenville's Proclamation of 1763, Sugar Act, Currency Act, and especially Stamp Act

7. The 1783 Treaty of Paris included which of the following agreements?
    a. Boundaries were established for the United States, including the southern tip of Florida as the southernmost boundary
    b. Britain was allowed to keep both Canada and Florida as imperial British territories under the terms of the Treaty of Paris
    c. The treaty stipulated that all private creditors in Britain were prohibited from making future debt collections from Americans
    d. Britain and the other most powerful countries of Europe recognized the United States' independence as a nation

8. Which of the following is not true with respect to the Constitutional Convention of 1787?
    a. The delegates to the Convention had a common opinion that people are inherently selfish
    b. Convention delegate Benjamin Franklin was quite instrumental in the Great Compromise
    c. Edmund Randolph designed the "Virginia Plan," which was introduced by James Madison
    d. Paterson's New Jersey Plan favoring smaller states was an alternative to the Virginia Plan

9. In what year was George Washington inaugurated as the first President of the United States?
    a. 1786
    b. 1787
    c. 1788
    d. 1789

10. Which of the following is a power held only by the federal government?
    a. The power to levy taxes, borrow money, and spend money
    b. The power to award copyrights and patents to people or groups
    c. The power to establish the criteria that qualify a person to vote
    d. The power to ratify proposed amendments to the Constitution

11. Which of the following was not a provision of the Judiciary Act of 1789?
    a. The initial establishment of the Supreme Court of the United States
    b. Constitutional validity of state laws to be judged by the Supreme Court
    c. The appointment of nine justices as members of the Supreme Court
    d. The establishment of a district court system for original jurisdiction

12. Which of the following is not a true statement regarding the Louisiana Purchase?
    a. Jefferson sent a delegation to Paris to endeavor to purchase only the city of New Orleans from Napoleon
    b. Napoleon, anticipating U.S. intrusions into Louisiana, offered to sell the U.S. the entire Louisiana territory
    c. The American delegation accepted Napoleon's offer, though they were only authorized to buy New Orleans
    d. The Louisiana Purchase, once it was completed, increased the territory of the U.S. by 50% overnight

13. Which of these was not a factor that contributed to the duel in which Aaron Burr killed Alexander Hamilton?
    a. Some Federalists who opposed U.S. Western expansion were attempting to organize a movement to secede from the Union
    b. Alexander Hamilton challenged Aaron Burr to a duel because he objected to U.S. expansion into the West, which Burr supported
    c. Secessionist Federalists tried to enlist Aaron Burr's support for their cause by backing him in his run for Governor of New York
    d. Alexander Hamilton was the leader of the group that opposed Aaron Burr's campaign to run for New York Governor

14. Which of these events was the least important contributing factor leading to the War of 1812?
    a. Macon's Bill No. 2 empowered the President to ban trade with any country that violated U.S. neutrality
    b. British officials running Canada were egging Indian tribes on in their border attacks of U.S. settlements
    c. The Spanish, who were allied with the British, were in favor of the Indian tribes' attacks on U.S. settlements
    d. The Non-Intercourse Act put an embargo on trade with Britain and France, but opened trade to other countries

15. Which of the following is not correct about the growth of America in the first half of the 19th century?
    a. By 1840, two thirds of all Americans resided west of the Allegheny Mountains
    b. The population of America doubled every 25 years during this time period
    c. The trend of westward expansion increased as more people migrated west
    d. Immigration to America from other countries was not substantial prior to 1820

16. Which of the following is not correct concerning the growth of American labor unions?
    a. The new factory system separated workers from owners, which tended to depersonalize workplaces
    b. The goal of attaining an 8-hour work day stimulated growth in labor organizing in the early 1800s
    c. The first organized workers' strike was in Paterson, New Jersey in 1828, and was by child laborers
    d. Recurring downturns in the economy tended to limit workers' demands for rights until the 1850s

17. Which of the following is not true regarding public schools in the early 19th century?
    a. Virtually no public schools existed in America prior to around 1815
    b. Schools were mainly financed by private corporate or religious groups
    c. Thomas Jefferson's plan of a free school in Virginia was realized
    d. American schools were elitist, catering to the rich and to males in academics

18. Which of the following was not an example of violence in cities that occurred as a result of rapid urbanization in America in the 1830s?
    a. Democrats opposed Whigs in New York City so strenuously that the state militia was called in
    b. Both New York City and Philadelphia experienced a series of racial riots during the mid-1830s
    c. A Catholic convent was attacked and plundered by a violent mob in New York City in 1834
    d. All of the above occurred in American cities during the 1830s

19. Which of the following is the most accurate description of the relationship between agriculture and industry in the 19th century?
    a. With industrial and technological advances, farming was left behind in favor of industrial work
    b. With more urban workers needing food, farming became more important than industrial work
    c. Specialization and mechanization were applied more to agriculture at this time than to industry
    d. The development of both agriculture and industry was helped by technological innovations

20. Which of the following statements is incorrect about U.S. westward expansion and Manifest Destiny?
    a. The idea that U.S. freedom and values should be shared with, even forced upon, as many people as possible had existed for many years
    b. The term "Manifest Destiny" and the idea it represented had been used for many years prior to the 1830s
    c. Many Americans believed that America as a nation should ultimately be extended to include Canada and Mexico
    d. Increased nationalism after the resolution of the War of 1812 and rapid population growth added to Manifest Destiny

21. Who negotiated the treaty that put an end to the Mexican War?
    a. USA President James K. Polk
    b. State Dept. clerk Nicholas Trist
    c. USA General Winfield Scott
    d. U.S. Colonel Stephen W. Kearny

22. Of the following events, which was the earliest precursor to the Vietnam War?
    a. The Truman administration financially supporting French imperialism
    b. Vietminh rebellion against the French
    c. The Eisenhower administration's financial support of the French cause
    d. The French signing of the Geneva Accords, which divided the country

23. Which of the following was least associated with actions President Ronald Reagan took against Communism in his administration?
    a. His reinforcement of America's military weaponry
    b. His Strategic Defense Initiative for space defenses
    c. His Reagan Doctrine supporting freedom fighters
    d. His withdrawal of Cuban troops from Angola

24. Which of the following was not a part of President George H.W. Bush's "New World Order," initiated between 1989-1992 and following the end of the Cold War?
    a. The START I and START II treaties signed by the US and Russia
    b. Government reform in Nicaragua and the end of civil war in El Salvador
    c. The signing of NAFTA by three countries and its ratification by the Senate
    d. All of these were actions taken by the Bush administration from 1989-1992

25. Of the following, which did not have a negative impact on the US economy after World War II?
    a. The Servicemen's Readjustment Act of 1944
    b. The demobilization of the US armed forces
    c. A decrease in defense manufacturing
    d. An increase in inflation rates

26. Which of the following statements regarding exceptions to postwar prosperity in 1960s America is not true?
    a. As of 1962, almost 15% of Americans had incomes at the government-defined poverty level
    b. The government-defined poverty level in 1962 was under $4,000 a year for a family of four
    c. Blacks in city ghettoes and Mexican American migrant workers made up major impoverished populations
    d. Native American Indians and whites living in Appalachia comprised major impoverished populations

27. Which of the following statements is not true regarding the events of September 11, 2001, in the US?

    a. Shortly after that date the US defeated the Taliban and captured Al-Qaeda leader Osama bin Laden

    b. On September 11, 2001, Muslim terrorists flew two hijacked airplanes into the World Trade Center in New York

    c. On September 11, 2001, Muslim terrorists flew a hijacked passenger airliner into the Pentagon in Arlington, Virginia

    d. An airplane hijacked by Muslim terrorists crashed in Pennsylvania after passengers resisted the terrorists

28. Which of the following rivers did not play an important role in the development of the earliest civilizations?

    a. The Tiber River
    b. The Yangtze River
    c. The Euphrates River
    d. The Nile River

29. Which of the following rulers was female?

    a. Sargon
    b. Hammurabi
    c. Hatshepsut
    d. Nebuchadnezzar

30. In what modern day country is the remains of Mesopotamian civilization found?

    a. Afghanistan
    b. Iraq
    c. Turkey
    d. Egypt

31. A monotheistic religious practice was central to which of the following cultures?

    a. Egyptians
    b. Hebrews
    c. Sumerians
    d. Babylonians

32. The first coin-based economy was established by which of the following people?

    a. Phoenicians
    b. Egyptians
    c. Hebrews
    d. Lydians

33. Which of the following refers to the slave class of ancient Sparta?

    a. Helots
    b. Hoplites
    c. Ephorate
    d. Metics

34. Which of the following is not a significant event in the Persian Wars?
    a. Persia invaded the Greek mainland
    b. Persians were driven back at the battle of Marathon
    c. The Greek forces vastly outnumbered the Persians
    d. The Persians attacked Athens

35. Which group overtook Rome in the mid-600s B.C. and established much of its infrastructure, including sewers, roads, and fortifications, only to be driven out of the city in 509 B.C.?
    a. Latins
    b. Etruscans
    c. Greeks
    d. Persians

36. Which of the following is not a reason why Europeans began colonizing other lands?
    a. They wanted to Christianize other peoples they viewed as savages
    b. Drought, famine, and war had destroyed most of Europe
    c. They needed to find additional sources of silver and gold to coin money
    d. They could establish new markets for goods produced in Europe

37. Which of the following is not part of triangular trade?
    a. Sailing from Europe to Africa
    b. Trading goods for slaves
    c. Selling the slaves to plantation owners in the Americas
    d. Trading American goods in Asia

38. What did the Scientific Revolution emphasize?
    a. Tradition and authority
    b. Observation and reason
    c. Superstition
    d. Theology

39. Of the following cultural developments influenced by the Catholic Church, which did not occur in the 14th and/or 15th centuries?
    a. Romanesque architecture
    b. Gothic architectural style
    c. Baroque arts, Jesuit order
    d. Renaissance works of art

40. The Renaissance which began in Italy subsequently spread to all but which of the following other countries in Europe?
    a. All of these
    b. France
    c. Germany
    d. England

41. Which of the following statements is true relative to the Protestant Reformation?
    a. The Magisterial Reformation and the Radical Reformation were not associated with the Protestant Reformation
    b. The Magisterial Reformation and the Radical Reformation were two different names for the same one movement
    c. The Magisterial Reformation and Radical Reformation were two sub-movements of the Protestant Reformation
    d. The Magisterial Reformation and the Radical Reformation took place during different historical periods of time

42. Which of the following statements does not characterize the Age of Absolutism?
    a. Nobles gained more power as monarchs had them live in their palaces
    b. The influence of the Church upon government diminished at this time
    c. The partitioning characteristic of feudal systems no longer took place
    d. All of these were characteristics found during the Age of Absolutism

43. Which of the following is not correct regarding assumptions of mercantilism?
    a. The money and the wealth of a nation are identical properties
    b. In order to prosper, a nation should try to increase its imports
    c. In order to prosper, a nation should try to increase its exports
    d. Economic protectionism by national governments is advisable

44. Which of the following is not true about the English Civil Wars between 1641 and 1651?
    a. These wars all were waged between Royalists and Parliamentarians
    b. The outcome of this series of civil wars was victory for Parliament
    c. These wars legalized Parliament's consent as requisite to monarchy
    d. Two of the wars in this time involved supporters of King Charles I

45. Which of the following choices is/are not considered among causes of the French Revolution?
    a. Famines causing malnutrition and starvation
    b. War debt, Court spending, bad monetary system
    c. Resentment against the Catholic Church's rule
    d. Resentment against the Protestant Reformation

46. Which of the following statements is accurate regarding the end of the First World War?
    a. The Treaty of Versailles brought peace among all countries involved in the war
    b. The Treaty of Versailles contained a clause for establishing the United Nations
    c. President Woodrow Wilson had proposed forming a coalition of world nations
    d. President Wilson succeeded in getting the USA to ratify the League of Nations

47. Which of the following empire(s) no longer existed following the armistice ending World War I?
    a. The Austro-Hungarian Empire
    b. The Ottoman Empire
    c. The German Empire
    d. All of these empires

48. Which of the following is not a true statement about the Second World War?
    a. It was a war wherein nations mobilized civilian as well as military resources
    b. It was a war wherein nations destroyed civilian as well as military personnel
    c. It eventually became known as "The War to End All Wars"
    d. It was the first war in history to detonate nuclear devices

49. Of the following countries, which did not experience more war soon after World War II?
    a. Greece
    b. China
    c. Korea
    d. Japan

50. Which of the following statements is true about post-World War II economic recovery various countries?
    a. About half the world's industrial production was by the United States
    b. West Germany, France, and the Soviet Union bounced back quickly
    c. Italy and China suffered postwar, but both countries recovered in a few years
    d. All of these statements are true about post-WWII economic recovery

51. Which of the following statements is not true about the American Colonization Society (A.C.S.) in the 1820s-1830s?
    a. It helped thousands of slaves to move to Africa where they could be free
    b. It helped thousands of free black people to move from America to Africa
    c. It was opposed by most abolitionists for repatriating but not emancipating
    d. It was the group responsible for founding the colony of Liberia, in Africa

52. During the decolonization of the Cold War years, which of the following events occurred chronologically latest?
    a. The Eastern Bloc and Satellite states became independent from the Soviet Union
    b. Canada became totally independent from British Parliament via the Canada Act
    c. The Bahamas, in the Caribbean, became independent from the United Kingdom
    d. The Algerian War ended, and Algeria became independent from France

53. Which of the following is not true about the Crusades?
    a. Their purpose was for European rulers to retake the Middle East from Muslims
    b. The Crusades succeeded at European kings' goal of reclaiming the "holy land"
    c. The Crusades accelerated the already incipient decline of the Byzantine Empire
    d. Egypt saw a return as a major Middle Eastern power as a result of the Crusades

54. During which of these periods were pyramids not built in Egypt?
    a. The Old Kingdom
    b. The Middle Kingdom
    c. The New Kingdom
    d. The Third Dynasty

55. Power divided between local and central branches of government is a definition of what term?
   a. Bicameralism
   b. Checks and balances
   c. Legislative oversight
   d. Federalism

56. The civil rights act that outlawed segregation in schools and public places also:
   a. Gave minorities the right to vote
   b. Established women's right to vote
   c. Outlawed unequal voter registration
   d. Provided protection for children

57. Which court case established the Court's ability to overturn laws that violated the Constitution?
   a. Miranda v. Arizona
   b. Marbury v. Madison
   c. United States v. Curtiss-Wright Export Corporation
   d. Brown v. Board of Education of Topeka

58. What judicial system did America borrow from England?
   a. Due process
   b. Federal law
   c. Commerce law
   d. Common law

59. To be President of the United States, one must meet these three requirements:
   a. The President must be college educated, at least 30 years old, and a natural citizen
   b. The President must be a natural citizen, have lived in the U.S. for 14 years, and have a college education
   c. The President must be a natural citizen, be at least 35 years old, and have lived in the U.S. for 14 years
   d. The President must be at least 30 years old, be a natural citizen, and have lived in the U.S. for 14 years

60. The Vice President succeeds the President in case of death, illness or impeachment. What is the order of succession for the next three successors, according to the Presidential Succession Act of 1947?
   a. President Pro Tempore of the Senate, Secretary of State, and Secretary of Defense
   b. Speaker of the House, President Pro Tempore of the Senate, and Secretary of State
   c. President Pro Tempore of the Senate, Speaker of the House, and Secretary of State
   d. Secretary of State, Secretary of Defense, and Speaker of the House

61. The President has the power to veto legislation. How is this power limited?
    I.   Congress can override the veto
    II. The President cannot line veto
    III. The President cannot propose legislation
       a. I and III
       b. II only
       c. I and II
       d. I only

62. What are the official requirements for serving in the House of Representatives?
    a. A member of the House must be at least 30 years old, a U.S. citizen for a minimum of nine years, and a resident of the state and district he represents
    b. A member of the House must be at least 25 years old, a natural citizen, and a resident of the state he represents
    c. A member of the House must be at least 30 years old, a natural citizen, and a resident of the state and district he represents
    d. A member of the House must be at least 25 years old, a U.S. citizen for a minimum of seven years, and a resident of the state he represents

63. What are the official requirements for becoming a Senator?
    a. A Senator must be at least 35 years old, a U.S. citizen for a minimum of seven years, and a resident of the state he represents
    b. A Senator must be at least 30 years old, a U.S. citizen for a minimum of nine years, and a resident of the state he represents
    c. A Senator must be at least 25 years old, a U.S. citizen for a minimum of nine years, and a resident of the state and district he represents
    d. A Senator must be at least 30 years old, a natural citizen, and a resident of the state he represents

64. How are members of the Federal Judiciary chosen?
    a. They are elected by voters
    b. They are appointed by the President and confirmed by the House of Representatives
    c. They are chosen by a committee
    d. They are appointed by the President and confirmed by the Senate

65. Parks and recreation services, police and fire departments, housing services, emergency medical services, municipal courts, transportation services, and public works usually fall under the jurisdiction of which body of government?
    a. State government
    b. Federal government
    c. Federal agencies
    d. Local government

66. How was the Vice President chosen before the 12th Amendment was ratified?
    a. The President chose the Vice President
    b. Congress chose the Vice President
    c. The Vice President came in second in the Electoral College
    d. There was no Vice President

67. What portion of the federal budget is dedicated to transportation, education, national resources, the environment, and international affairs?
    a. Mandatory spending
    b. Discretionary spending
    c. Undistributed offsetting receipts
    d. Official budget outlays

68. Who negotiates treaties?
    a. The President
    b. The House of Representatives
    c. Ambassadors
    d. The Senate

69. What is the term for the general agreement on fundamental principles of governance and the values supporting them?
    a. Rule of law
    b. Nationalism
    c. Political culture
    d. Democratic consensus

70. What do the American labor union movement, the antislavery movement, the women's suffrage movement, and the civil rights movement have in common?
    a. They all used political protest
    b. They all appealed to legal precedent
    c. They all came from political homogeneity
    d. They were all protected by the commerce clause

71. Gun control, strong environmental laws, social programs, and opposition to the death penalty are what kind of issues?
    a. Compassion issues
    b. Activism
    c. Regional issues
    d. Religious issues

72. What group petitions the government?
    a. Common Cause
    b. Party leaders
    c. Lobbyists
    d. Party activists

73. Which supranational institution regulates international trade, human rights, and nation development?
    a. The UN
    b. The EEOC
    c. The UNDP
    d. The GOP

74. What was an early difference between Marxism and fascism?
    a. Fascism came out of socialism and Marxism from capitalism
    b. Fascists were nationalists and Marxists had an international focus
    c. Fascists wanted to defeat capitalism and Marxists wanted to preserve private property
    d. Marxism originally wanted to preserve class structure and fascism supported capitalism

75. Modern separation of powers preserves which principle?
    a. Mixed government
    b. Democracy
    c. Parliamentary system
    d. Presidential system

76. What institution affiliated with the UN is responsible for stabilizing foreign exchange rates?
    a. UNDP
    b. IMF
    c. EEOC
    d. PLEO

77. What kind of nation is made up of special interest groups focused on the civil liberties influencing public policy?
    a. Fascist
    b. Communist
    c. Pluralist
    d. Socialist

78. What do Marxists and capitalists have in common?
    a. They both believe in privatizing land ownership
    b. They both support free international trade
    c. They both support nationalization of the private sector
    d. They both support special interest groups

79. Authoritarian regimes often have which type of legislature?
    a. Bicameral
    b. Unicameral
    c. Multi-cameral
    d. Representative

80. Which constitutional requirement for passing a bill rarely happens?
    a. The leader of the majority party decides when to place the bill on the calendar for consideration before Congress
    b. The versions of a bill that pass through both houses of Congress and are signed by the President must have the exact same wording
    c. The number and kind of amendments introduced in the House are limited
    d. A filibuster needs a supermajority vote to be broken

81. Delegates awarded to Puerto Rico, Guam, and American Samoa in the Democratic National Convention are:
    a. PLEO delegates
    b. Base delegates
    c. District delegates
    d. Bonus delegates

82. The shortest distance between New York and Paris goes
    a. over Florida and Spain
    b. along the 42nd parallel
    c. over Labrador and Greenland
    d. over Philadelphia and London

83. On which type of map are different countries represented in different colors, with no two adjacent countries sharing a color?
    a. Physical map
    b. Political map
    c. Climate map
    d. Contour map

84. On a map of Africa, there is a small box around Nairobi. This city is depicted in greater detail in a box at the bottom of the map. What is the name for this box at the bottom of the map?
    a. Inset
    b. Legend
    c. Compass Rose
    d. Key

85. Which map describes the movement of people, trends, or materials across a physical area?
    a. Political Map
    b. Cartogram
    c. Qualitative Map
    d. Flow-line Map

86. Antarctica will appear the largest on a
    a. Mercator projection
    b. Robinson projection
    c. Homolosine projection
    d. Azimuthal projection

87. Which type of chart is best at representing the cycle of demographic transition?
    a. Pie chart
    b. Political map
    c. Line graph
    d. Flow-line map

88. Which part of a hurricane features the strongest winds and greatest rainfall?
   a. Eye wall
   b. Front
   c. Eye
   d. Outward spiral

89. Which type of rock is formed by extreme heat and pressure?
   a. Limestone
   b. Metamorphic
   c. Sedimentary
   d. Igneous

90. What is the name for a brief interval of coolness in between warm periods in the Pacific Ocean?
   a. La Niña
   b. Tropical gyre
   c. El Niño
   d. ENSO

91. The rocks and landmasses that make up the earth's surface are called the
   a. atmosphere
   b. biosphere
   c. hydrosphere
   d. lithosphere

92. In the plate movement known as ____, an oceanic plate slides underneath a continental plate.
   a. faulting
   b. spreading
   c. subduction
   d. converging

93. Which of the following is an example of chemical weathering?
   a. Frost wedging
   b. Heat expansion
   c. Acid rain
   d. Salt wedging

94. Thai food has become increasingly popular in the United States, though it is prepared in slightly different ways here. This is an example of
   a. Cultural Divergence
   b. Assimilation
   c. Cultural convergence
   d. Acculturation

95. Which of the following is not one of the necessary characteristics of a geographical region?
    a. Area
    b. Location
    c. Homogeneity
    d. Population

96. Which of the following is not one of the demographic variables?
    a. Fertility
    b. Diversity
    c. Mortality
    d. Migration

97. Which of the following is an example of indirect diffusion?
    a. The Dutch and the Belgians both love soccer
    b. Iran forbids its citizens from watching Western television programs
    c. Japanese anime comics are popular in the United States
    d. Many Native Americans have struggled with alcoholism

98. Which of the following is a true statement about the Yucatan Peninsula?
    a. It is densely populated
    b. It is more mountainous than the rest of Mexico
    c. It was once inhabited by Aztecs
    d. It has a number of large sinkholes

99. After the United States, which of the following nations imports the most oil?
    a. China
    b. Brazil
    c. Germany
    d. Japan

100. Which of the following is not an official language of Switzerland?
    a. Italian
    b. Dutch
    c. French
    d. German

101. Which two nations share the longest undefended border in the world?
    a. Chile and Argentina
    b. Canada and the United States
    c. Kazakhstan and Russia
    d. Egypt and Sudan

102. Assume a society has a given production possibilities frontier (PPF) representing the production of guns and butter. Which of the following would cause the PPF to move outward?
    a. The invention of a new machine that makes guns more efficiently
    b. An increase in the production of butter
    c. An increase in the production of guns
    d. A decrease in the production of guns and butter

103. A society produces 10 units of Good X and 10 units of Good Y. Then, the society changes its production, increasing production of Good X to 15 units. Production of Good Y drops to 6 units. What is the opportunity cost of producing the additional 5 units of Good X?
   a. 5 units of Good X
   b. 15 units of Good X
   c. 6 units of Good Y
   d. 4 units of Good Y

Question 104 pertains to the following production possibilities for the United States and Mexico:

Production in United States

Corn (bushels)	100	80	60	40	20	0
Oil (gallons)	0	20	40	60	80	100

Production in Mexico

Corn (bushels)	0	10	20	30	40	50
Oil (gallons)	25	20	15	10	5	0

104. Which of the following statements is false?
   a. The United States has an absolute advantage in corn production
   b. The United States has an absolute advantage in oil production
   c. The United States has an absolute advantage in both corn and oil production
   d. The United States has a comparative advantage in corn production

105. Which of the following are true of the demand curve?
   I.   It is normally downward sloping
   II.   It is normally upward sloping
   III. It is influenced by the law of diminishing marginal unity
   IV.   It is unaffected by the law of diminishing marginal unity
   a. I and III only
   b. I and IV only
   c. II and III only
   d. II and IV only

106. Which of the following would not increase aggregate demand (AD)?
   a. Government spending increases, while taxes stay the same
   b. Consumer confidence about the economy grows
   c. US government cuts defense spending dramatically while holding domestic spending steady
   d. The US government cuts taxes

107. Assume that aggregate demand is at AD1 and the government borrows money and then spends that money in order to attempt to move aggregate demand to AD3. According to the theory of "crowding out," where is AD likely to wind up?

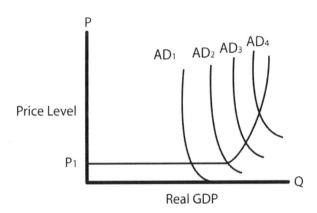

a. AD1
b. AD2
c. AD3
d. AD4

108. Which of the following statements about the long run aggregate supply (LRAS) curve is correct?
a. The horizontal part represents high levels of unemployment
b. The curved part represents high levels of unemployment
c. The vertical part represents high levels of unemployment
d. The LRAS curve is a straight, vertical line

109. Assume that the FOMC purchases bonds. Which of the following will happen?
a. The money supply increases, bond yields decline, bond interest rates decline
b. The money supply increases, bond yields increase, bond interest rates decline
c. The money supply increases, bond yields decline, bond interest rates increase
d. The money supply increases, bond yields increase, bond interest rates increase

110. What measures the impact of choosing one option over another?
a. Supply
b. Elasticity
c. Comparative advantage
d. Opportunity cost

111. Miguel and Huan both work at a software company. In one hour, Miguel can create one computer graphic or write ten pages of text. In the same hour, Huan can create three computer graphics or write 20 pages of text. Based on this information, it can be said that:
    a. Miguel has an absolute advantage in creating computer graphics
    b. Miguel has an absolute advantage in writing pages of text
    c. Miguel has a comparative advantage in creating computer graphics
    d. Miguel has a comparative advantage in writing text

112. Ciao Bella Pizza faces this production function when making pizzas:

Pizzas Produced	Total Cost
0	0
1	6
2	12
3	18
4	23
5	28
6	32
7	37
8	43

Which pizza has the lowest marginal cost?
    a. First
    b. Third
    c. Sixth
    d. Seventh

113. Which of the following statements about the production possibilities frontier are correct?
    I.   Points on the frontier are efficient
    II.   Points inside the line are efficient
    III.   Points outside the line are unattainable
    IV.   The frontier represents all possible production combinations of all goods
    a. I and IV
    b. II and III
    c. I and III
    d. II and IV

114. What does the distinctive, outwardly bowed shape of the PPF signify?
    a. The law of supply and demand
    b. The efficiency of the free market system
    c. That the two goods do not have constant opportunity costs when producing in different quantities along the PPF
    d. The unequal distribution of wealth within a society

115. John is considering using $100 dollars to download $100 worth of music, buy $100 worth of video games, or contribute $100 to charity. Which of the following statements correctly defines the opportunity cost of his decision?
  a. If John buys music, the opportunity cost is the lost opportunity to buy video games and contribute to charity
  b. If John contributes to charity, there is no opportunity cost
  c. If John contributes to charity, the opportunity cost is the lost opportunity to buy music and video games
  d. If John buys video games, the opportunity cost can be defined as the lost opportunity to buy music or donate to charity

116. The price of fleece blankets goes up from $10 to $11. At the same time, demand goes down from 1,000 blankets to 800 blankets. Which of the following statements is true?
  a. Demand is elastic
  b. Demand is inelastic
  c. The price elasticity quotient, or E_d, is less than 1
  d. The price elasticity quotient, or E_d, is equal to 1

117. Which of the following statements about price elasticity of supply is not correct?
  a. If the percentage change in the quantity supplied is greater than the percentage change in price, the supply is elastic
  b. The supply of a good or service with a short life expectancy, such as fresh grapes, is inelastic
  c. Short-run supply for a factory producing a good through a complicated combination of resources tends to be inelastic
  d. If E_s is greater than 1, supply is inelastic

Question 118 pertains to the following graph:

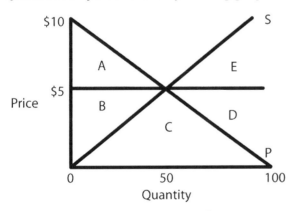

118. Which of the following areas represents consumer surplus?
  a. A
  b. B
  c. C
  d. D

119.
    I.   The demand curve shifts to the right
    II.   The equilibrium price increases
    III.   The equilibrium quantity increases
    IV.   The supply curve shifts to the left
A determinant of demand increases. What follows?
    a. Only I
    b. I and II only
    c. I, II, and III only
    d. I, II, III, and IV

Question 120 pertains to the following graph:

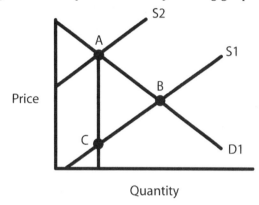

120. Assume a government places a tax on books. Which area on the map above represents the deadweight loss that results from that tax?
    a. The area bounded by points A, B, and C
    b. The area left of S2 and above E2
    c. The area between S1 and S2
    d. The area right of S2

Answers and Explanations

1. B: The Virginia Company of London was based in London, not Massachusetts. It had a charter to colonize American land between the Hudson and Cape Fear rivers (c). The other Virginia Company was the Virginia Company of Plymouth, which was based in the American colony of Plymouth, Massachusetts (a). It had a charter to colonize North America between the Potomac River and the northern boundary of Maine (d).

2. C: The Pilgrims were not Puritans seeking to escape religious persecution in England. They were actually English Separatists (d) who believed there was no fixing the Church of England, and thus chose to separate from it. They did embark on the *Mayflower* in 1620, and storms drove the ship to land at Cape Cod, Massachusetts (a). Their leader was William Bradford, and they had been given a charter by the London Company to settle America (b) south of the Hudson River. The Pilgrims knew that going ashore would leave them without any existing government, so while still on board the ship they created the Mayflower Compact so that their New World colony would have a basis for government from its inception.

3. D: While it is true that British mercantilism, used partly as a weapon against Holland, did contribute to three wars between Britain and Holland in the late 17th century, it is not true that mercantilism never contributed to colonial prosperity. It did contribute to the wealth of the New England colonies by supporting their active ship building industry. Conversely, mercantilism was harmful to the Chesapeake colonies because it lowered prices on tobacco crops, their main source of income. According to English mercantilism, economic enterprises should always be government controlled (a). As subjects of the British Empire, American colonies definitely contributed to the mercantilist system by farming many crops that the England could take advantage of (b) instead of having to import them from foreign countries. To enforce colonial supply of crops to England, Parliament passed the Navigation Acts from 1651 to 1673 (c).

4. B: King William's War, which was fought between 1689 and 1697, included quite a few violent border attacks by Indians in America, but no major army battles. The Treaty of Ryswick ending this war did not make any changes in territories. Queen Anne's War (a), which lasted from 1702 to 1713, was fought against France and Spain. It was ended by the Treaty of Utrecht, which ceded much territory to England. King George's War (c), which lasted from 1739 to 1748, involved major army battles on American soil. American soldiers went on a number of expeditions with British troops. The Treaty of Aix-la-Chapelle ended this war. In it, England returned Louisbourg to France, trading it for territories on the Indian continent. The French and Indian War (d), which lasted from 1754 to 1763, featured many army battles on American soil. The 1763 Treaty of Paris ending this war ceded all of France's territories in Canada and North America to England.

5. D: Among American political philosophers and writers who embraced the Enlightenment, Benjamin Franklin was the most famous. It is not true that this movement began in America and spread to Europe (a). On the contrary, it developed simultaneously in many European countries, and then spread to America. It is not true that the importance of God in the world was one of its central premises (b). The Enlightenment was a rationalist movement. According to its philosophy, the application of human critical thinking had more importance in solving problems than any divine intervention. It is not true that John Locke, a major British Enlightenment figure, believed governments should not be deposed for violating

social or political rights (c). He believed the opposite: that if a government did not allow its citizens such rights, it was a valid reason to overthrow that government. This kind of thinking is also seen in the Enlightenment belief of challenging a society's traditional moral values, practices, and existing institutions rather than always upholding them.

6. A: The attitudes of American colonists after the 1763 Treaty of Paris ended the French and Indian War was not a direct contributor to the American Revolution. American colonists had a supportive attitude toward Great Britain then, and were proud of the part they played in winning the war. Their good will was not returned by British leaders (b), who looked down on American colonials and sought to increase their imperial power over them. Even in 1761, a sign of Americans' objections to having their liberty curtailed by the British was seen when Boston attorney James Otis argued in court against the Writs of Assistance (c), search warrants to enforce England's mercantilist trade restrictions, as violating the kinds of natural laws espoused during the Enlightenment. Lord George Grenville's aggressive program to defend the North American frontier in the wake of Chief Pontiac's attacks included stricter enforcement of the Navigation Acts, the Proclamation of 1763, the Sugar Act (or Revenue Act), the Currency Act, and most of all the Stamp Act (d). Colonists objected to these as taxation without representation. Other events followed in this taxation dispute, which further eroded Americans' relationship with British government, including the Townshend Acts, the Massachusetts Circular Letter, the Boston Massacre, the Tea Act, and the resulting Boston Tea Party. Finally, with Britain's passage of the Intolerable Acts and the Americans' First Continental Congress, which was followed by Britain's military aggression against American resistance, actual warfare began in 1775. While not all of the colonies wanted war or independence by then, things changed by 1776, and Jefferson's Declaration of Independence was formalized. James Otis, Samuel Adams, Patrick Henry, the Sons of Liberty, and the Stamp Act Congress also contributed to the beginning of the American Revolution.

7. D: The Treaty of Paris of 1783 did state that Britain and the other leading European countries now recognized the United States of America as an independent country. This treaty also set boundaries, but the southern tip of Florida was not the southern boundary (a). It was the northern boundary of Florida, which became a Spanish territory. Therefore, it is not true that Britain kept both Canada and Florida under this treaty (b). Canada did remain a British territory under its terms, but Britain had to cede Florida to Spain. The Treaty of Paris also gave private British creditors freedom to collect debts from Americans, not the reverse (c). The treaty also stipulated that property confiscated from loyalists during the war should be given back, not kept. Other terms of the Treaty of Paris included that the western boundary of the United States would be the Mississippi River.

8. C: James Madison was the one who designed the Virginia Plan. Edmund Randolph, a more proficient public speaker, introduced this plan at Madison's request—not the other way around. It is true that the Convention delegates believed that humans are basically selfish by nature (a), which was why they instituted checks and balances in the constitution to keep the government or any part of it from abusing its powers or acquiring too much power. Benjamin Franklin was instrumental in the Great Compromise (b), which was reached with his help after the convention went into deadlock over choosing the Virginia Plan or the New Jersey Plan. The New Jersey Plan, designed by William Paterson, was offered as an alternative to the Virginia Plan (d), as it would give smaller states equal influence as larger states. The Great Compromise incorporated elements of both plans by having the equal representation outlined in the New Jersey Plan in the Senate and the representation based

on population outlined in the Virginia Plan in the House of Representatives. The Three-Fifths Compromise was reached to resolve differences between Northern and Southern states over the issue of slavery. Each slave was counted as three-fifths of a person for representation and taxation purposes.

9. D: George Washington was inaugurated as the first President of the United States in March of 1789, following the completion of each state's ratification of the Constitution. 1786 (a) was the year the Annapolis Convention met with the aim of changing the Articles of Confederation. Because only five states sent delegates, however, those officiating decided it would be better to arrange for a convention the following summer, which delegates representing all states would attend. This became known as the Constitutional Convention, which met in 1787 (b). The minimum requirement of ratification of the Constitution by nine of the thirteen states was achieved in 1788 (c).

10. B: Only the federal government has the power to give copyrights and patents to individuals or companies. The power to levy taxes, borrow money, and spend money (a) is a power shared by federal and state governments. The power to set the criteria that qualify individuals to vote (c) is a power given to state governments only. The power to ratify amendments proposed to the Constitution (d) is a power of only the state governments.

11. C: The Judiciary Act of 1789 did not include the appointment of nine justices of the Supreme Court. The original Supreme Court only had six justices. The Judiciary Act of 1789 did initially establish the Supreme Court (a). This act stated that Supreme Court Justices were to make rulings about whether state laws were constitutionally valid (b). The Judiciary Act also stipulated that a system of district courts be set up as courts of original jurisdiction (d), and it allowed for the establishment of three courts of appeal.

12. D: The Louisiana Purchase actually increased the U.S.'s territory by 100% overnight, not 50%. The Louisiana territory doubled the size of the nation. It is true that Jefferson initially sent a delegation to Paris to see if Napoleon would agree to sell only New Orleans to the United States (a). It is also true that Napoleon, who expected America to encroach on Louisiana, decided to avoid this by offering to sell the entire territory to the U.S. (b). It is likewise true that America only had authority to buy New Orleans. Nevertheless, the delegation accepted Napoleon's offer of all of Louisiana (c). Due to his belief in strict interpretation of the Constitution, Jefferson did require approval from Congress to make the purchase. When his advisors characterized the purchase as being within his purview based on the presidential power to make treaties, Congress agreed.

13. B: Hamilton did not object to U.S. western expansionism, and Burr did not support it. There were certain Federalists other than Hamilton who opposed expansion to the west as a threat to their position within the Union, and these opponents did attempt to organize a movement to secede (a). To get Aaron Burr to champion their cause, they offered to help him run for Governor of New York (c). Hamilton did lead the opposition against Burr's campaign (d).

14. D: The Non-Intercourse Act passed by Congress, which opened trade to all countries other than Britain and France, expired in 1810. It was succeeded by Macon's Bill No. 2 (a), which empowered the President to ban trade with any country that violated U.S. neutrality, and was thus more directly influential to the war. In 1810 and 1811, Indian tribes attacking U.S. settlements at the borders received encouragement from both British officials in

Canada (b) and from Spain (c), one of Britain's allies. Henry Clay and John C. Calhoun were leaders of the War Hawks, a pro-war group. In 1811, they gained control of both the Senate and the House of Representatives, and pushed to declare war against Britain. By June 1, 1812, President Madison asked Congress to declare war, which it did.

15. A: By 1840, more than one third of all Americans lived west of the Alleghenies, but not two thirds. It is correct that in the first half of the 19th century, the American population doubled every 25 years (b). It is also correct that westward expansion increased as more people moved west (c) during these years. It is correct that there was not a lot of immigration to the U.S. from other countries before 1820 (d).

16. B: Growth in labor organizing was stimulated by organizers wanting to achieve the goal of a shorter workday. However, what they were aiming for in the 1800s was a 10-hour day, not an 8-hour day, which was not realized until 1936. It is true that when the factory system supplanted the cottage industry, owners and workers became separate, and this depersonalized workplaces (a). Child laborers did conduct the first organized workers' strike in Paterson, N.J., in 1828 (c). Although the first strike did occur this early, there were not a lot of strikes or labor negotiations during this time period due to periodic downturns in the economy (d), which had the effect of keeping workers dependent and less likely to take action against management.

17. C: Thomas Jefferson did describe a plan for Virginia to have a free school, but it was not realized. Jefferson's plan was never implemented. It is true that there were really no public schools worth mentioning in America before around 1815 (a). Once there were schools, they were mainly paid for by private organizations – corporate ones in the Northeastern states and religious ones in the Southern and Mid-Atlantic states (b). America's early schools did cater to rich people, and specialized in providing academic instruction to males (d). The few schools for females in existence taught homemaking and fine arts rather than academic subjects. The New York Free School was a very unusual instance of an early American school that provided education for the poor. This school tried out the Lancastrian system, wherein older students tutor younger students, which not only employed a sound educational principle, but also helped the school to operate within its limited budget.

18. D: All of these are examples of urban violence in 1830s America. Political differences between Democrats and Whigs in New York City escalated into such violent fighting that the state militia was called in to subdue the disagreeing parties (a). Race riots broke out in New York City and Philadelphia during this decade (b). An angry mob in New York even went so far as to raid a Catholic convent in 1834 (c). City records counted 115 major incidents of mob violence during this decade. All of these events were attributable to the very rapid influx of people to the cities, causing mob violence and street crime to grow out of control.

19. D: Advances in technology were applied not only to industrial production, but also to farming machinery. Farmers could then supply larger amounts of food to urban workers at lower prices. Farming was not abandoned in favor of industry (a). The many additional workers in cities needed food that they did not grow, so there was an even greater market for farming. This did not mean that farming took precedence over industry (b). Both fields increased during the 19th century, and they complemented one another. Specialization and mechanization were processes applied to both farming and industry. At this time, they were not applied more to farming (c) or industry.

20. B: The term "Manifest Destiny" had not been used for many years before the 1830s. This term was coined in 1844. However, it is true that the idea this term expressed had been around for many years before that (a). It is also true that many Americans believed Manifest Destiny would mean America would ultimately encompass Canada and Mexico (c). Factors contributing to Manifest Destiny included the rise in nationalism that followed the War of 1812 and the population growth that increased that nationalism (d). Other factors that contributed to Manifest Destiny included the 1830s' reform movements and the demand for additional markets and resources created by the growth of the economy.

21. B: The Treaty of Guadalupe-Hidalgo, signed on February 2, 1848, was negotiated by a clerk for the State Department, Nicholas Trist (b). This was done even though Trist had had his authority revoked and been ordered to return to Washington two months before that date. President Polk (a) did not negotiate this treaty and felt that its terms were too generous. He accepted it, however, and it was then ratified by the Senate. General Winfield Scott (c) was ordered by President Polk to capture Mexico City when Mexico's government refused negotiations even after the success of Polk's three-pronged attack. Scott defeated Mexican forces at Veracruz, Cerro Gordo, Churubusco, the fortress at Chapultepec, and finally at Mexico City. Colonel Stephen Kearny (d) had led the first prong of Polk's three-pronged attack, taking New Mexico and then advancing to California. In the second prong, Commodore Robert Stockton brought his men ashore to join Kearny's men, and together they defeated Mexican soldiers at the Battle of San Gabriel in January of 1847, completing California's occupation.

22. B: The Communist Ho Chi Minh led the Vietminh rebellion against French efforts to colonize Vietnam in 1946. Truman's administration gave monetary support to French colonizers (a) starting in 1950. Following Truman's office, Eisenhower's administration also financially supported French imperialism (c). France signed the Geneva Accords, creating a temporary division between North and South Vietnam (d), in 1954. North Vietnam was given to Ho Chi Minh while South Vietnam was given to Bao Dai, who was backed by the French. Initially the US supported Ngo Dinh Diem in deposing Bao Dai because American leaders thought this would prevent Vietnam falling under Communist control. However, once in power, Diem became corrupt and dictatorial, leading to South Vietnamese resistance against his reign.

23. D: The action least associated with Reagan's anti-Communist measures was (d), his withdrawal of Cuban troops from Angola in 1988. This troop withdrawal was in answer to pressure to force an end to South Africa's apartheid policies, which segregated blacks from whites. The US levied economic sanctions against South Africa in 1986, after "constructive engagement" efforts failed to end apartheid. In 1988, the Reagan administration negotiated to allow black majority rule in Namibia and to remove Cuban troops from Angola. Therefore answer (d) is a reflection of anti-apartheid actions rather than anti-Communist actions. In efforts to protect the US from Communism, Reagan reinforced our systems of military weaponry (a). He introduced the Strategic Defense Initiative to establish antimissile systems in space (b). In addition, he announced his "Reagan Doctrine," which granted American support to freedom fighters who resisted communist rule (c).

24. D: All of these were actions taken by the Bush administration between 1989-1992, is correct. In 1991, the US and Russia signed the START I treaty, and in 1992, they signed the START II treaty (a). Both of these treaties were agreements by both countries to decrease their arsenals of nuclear weapons. In 1989, the US invaded Panama and overthrew Dictator

Manuel Noriega while supporting the National Opposition Union there, which won the 1990 election against the Sandinista Front; and in 1992, US diplomacy ended the civil war in El Salvador (b). Also in 1992, the US signed the North American Free Trade Agreement (NAFTA) with Canada and Mexico, and the US Senate ratified it in 1994, (c). This agreement provided for trading relations among these countries that were mostly free of tariffs. The Persian Gulf War resulted from Iraq's invasion of Kuwait in 1990. Bush intervened with the US Air Force in January of 1991, and within a month he mobilized the Army, Marine Corps, Navy, and Coast Guard to Saudi Arabia, subsequently invading Iraq. At Bush's encouragement, other countries also sent troops there. These combined forces moved the Iraqis out of Kuwait in four days. The UN Security Council approved a cease-fire in April 1991; a hundred days after the ground forces were deployed. Additional actions by Bush during this period included sending troops to Somalia in 1992 to manage the distribution of humanitarian aid and assigning a UN peacekeeping force in 1993 to assume this duty.

25. A: The event that did not have a negative impact on the postwar US economy was (a) the Servicemen's Readjustment Act of 1944, or Public Law 78-346. More familiarly called the GI Bill, this law gave financial aid for education to former soldiers. More than a million war veterans went to college on the GI Bill. This was one economic advantage among a number of disadvantages. Demobilization of the armed forces (b) took place quickly, such that from 1945 to 1947, the numbers in the military were reduced to one quarter of their previous count, from 12 million to 3 million, putting a great strain on the economy. With war supplies no longer needed, the defense manufacturing industry was reduced (c), so by 1946, rates of unemployment had risen to more than 2.5 million people. The Office of Price Administration removed wartime controls on prices, and Americans began spending money they had saved during the war, resulting in an increase in inflation (d) to 18% by 1946. Many unionized laborers found their work hours and wages, reduced after the war, leading to a proliferation of union strikes. When the United Mine Workers went on strike in 1946, President Truman ordered a temporary seizure by the government of the coal mines and threatened repeats of this action.

26. A: As of 1962, almost **25%** (not 15%) of Americans had poverty-level incomes (less than $4,000 a year for a family of four) (b). The least prosperous segments of the population were black people living in ghettoes of the inner cities; Mexican American migrant farm workers; Native American Indians; white people living in Appalachia; and elderly Americans who could not get Social Security benefits. The proportion of poor people in an affluent nation was brought to light by Michael Harrington in his 1962 book *The Other America.*

27. A: It is not true that the US defeated the Taliban and captured Osama bin Laden shortly after 9/11/2001. Osama bin Laden was killed during a raid on a private compound in Pakistan in 2011, nearly 10 years after the attacks. It is true that Muslim terrorists flew two of the four American airplanes they had hijacked into the twin towers of the World Trade Center in New York City (b). They flew the third of the four planes into the US Department of Defense's headquarters, the Pentagon building in Arlington, Virginia, (c) near Washington, D.C. The fourth plane crashed in a field near Shanksville, Pennsylvania, after some of the passengers on board tried to overtake the terrorists (d). President George W. Bush announced a "war on terrorism" after these attacks killed a total of 2,995 people.

28. C:This passage contains two clues to the answer: one the river flows north and two the river lies to the south of the Mediterranean Sea. The Nile is the only river listed that flows

south-to-north and lies to the south of the Mediterranean, making (C: the best choice. These geographical clues can be used to exclude the other choices: the Tiber is incorrect because it lies to the north of the Mediterranean Sea. The other choices are incorrect because these rivers lie east or southeast of the sea.

29. C: Hatshepsut was an Egyptian Pharaoh whose name means "foremost of noble ladies." Sargon, Hammurabi, Nebuchadnezzar, and Amenhotep IV were men.

30. B: is correct. Mesopotamian civilization developed in the Tigris and Euphrates River Valley, an area now controlled by Iraq. None of the other answers accurately reflects the geography of the region.

31. B: Of the cultures listed, only the Hebrews worshipped one God. Egyptians, Sumerians, Babylonians, and Hittites all practiced polytheistic religions that worshipped a host of deities.

32. D: Around 600 B.C., the Lydians of Asia Minor were one of the first to coin metal currency.

33. A: Members of the slave class of ancient Sparta were called helots. Hoplites, refers to a type of foot soldier. The ephorate was a governing body in Sparta. Metics is a term that refers to a class of people living in Athens who were not Athenian citizens by birth and who could not own land or run for political office. Archon refers to a governing body in Athens that assumed the duties of the former kings.

34. C: Each of the statements is true except C. The historical record indicates the Greeks were outnumbered by the Persians many times over. Persian forces did invade the Greek mainland in retaliation for Athens' involvement in an uprising against Persian Satraps in Asia Minor. Greek soldiers did repel the Persian army at the battle of Marathon. Persian forces did penetrate the Greek's defenses and sack Athens. Athens and Sparta did align themselves against Persia in their defense of the Greek mainland.

35. B: The Etruscans were from a kingdom to the north that seized control of Rome from the Latins in the mid-600s B.C. They began urbanizing the settlement, improving roads, adding drainage systems, etc. They were driven out of the region in 509 B.C. during an uprising of the Latins.

36. B: While much drought, famine, and war took place in Europe, none of these events completely destroyed the region. Many people remained in Europe despite expansion abroad.

37. D: Triangular trade refers to the process by which Europeans exchanged goods and slaves with the Americas.

38. B: The Scientific Revolution emphasized careful observation of the natural world and applied reason to make and test generalizations about how it operated. The Scientific Revolution saw its zenith in the wide-ranging discoveries of Sir Isaac Newton (1642-1727:.

39. C: The cultural development that did not occur in the 14th and/or 15th centuries was the Baroque style in the arts (music, visual arts, architecture). The Baroque arts were

- 133 -

encouraged by the Church during the Counter-Reformation, which occurred following the beginning of the Protestant Reformation as a reaction against it, in the 16th century. In addition, the Jesuit order was formed during this time (as well as other religious orders such as the Theatines and the Barnabites). The Jesuits quickly assumed a leading role in educating people during the Counter-Reformation. Romanesque architecture (a) developed out of the influence of the Catholic Church between circa 1000 and circa 1300, when it was succeeded by the Gothic style (b), also influenced by the Church and its cathedrals. The Catholic Church also sponsored most of the great artists of the Renaissance (d), including Michelangelo, Leonardo Da Vinci, Raphael, Botticelli, Bernini, Titian, Caravaggio, Tintoretto, Fra Angelico and their famous paintings and sculptures, during the 14th and 15th centuries. The Catholic Church was also responsible for the development of European classical music because Catholic monks pioneered the first modern system of musical notation in order to standardize religious music the world over. This innovation not only allowed for the composition of a vast body of liturgical music, but also it contributed to the development of secular classical music in Europe.

40. A: All of these countries experienced their own Renaissances following the Italian Renaissance, which began in the cities of Florence and Siena and spread through Italy. From there the intellectual and cultural developments of the period spread to France (b) from the late 15th to early 17th century, to Germany (c) in the 15th and 16th centuries, to England (d) from the early 16th to early 17th century, and to Poland from the late 15th to late 16th century, as well as to the Netherlands in the 16th century, in a movement often known as the Northern Renaissance. This name distinguishes it from the original Italian Renaissance.

41. D: All of these traditions evolved out of the Protestant Reformation. The Lutheran (a) tradition is named for Martin Luther, who began the Protestant Reformation with his 95 Theses, and the Lutheran tradition is known by the same name as a denomination of Protestant Christianity. The Anglican (b) tradition often has been called "Church of England," for the church with which it was originally associated. The Anglican Church became known in America as the Episcopal Church when America declared independence from England, since the original Anglican prayer books contained prayers for the British Royal Family. In Canada, it still was known as the Church of England, although in both the United States and Canada the new Anglican churches had separation of church and state. The Reformed (c) tradition includes such denominations as Calvinist, Presbyterian, and many other current denominations. Calvinism was originally the chief source of doctrine for all Reformed groups, and although this is no longer true of all current churches in the Reformed tradition, Calvinism still represents the orientation of most Reformed churches.

42. A: Nobles did not gain more power during the Age of Absolutism. Though the monarchs of that period often did require nobility to live in their royal palaces, this practice brought the nobility less power rather than more power, since it forced the nobles into dependence upon the monarchs for their income while officials of the state governed the noblemen's lands. In addition to the nobility, the Church also experienced a loss of influence (b) during this period as the monarch and the state gained more power, and state laws were developed. Partitioning common under the feudal system no longer took place (c) as most or all of the power was consolidated to the monarch.

43. B: In order to prosper, a nation should not try to increase its imports. Mercantilism is an economic theory including the idea that prosperity comes from a positive balance of international trade. For any one nation to prosper, that nation should increase its exports

(c) but decrease its imports. Exporting more to other countries while importing less from them will give a country a positive trade balance. This theory assumes that money and wealth are identical (a) assets of a nation. In addition, this theory also assumes that the volume of global trade is an unchangeable quantity. Mercantilism dictates that a nation's government should apply a policy of economic protectionism (d) by stimulating more exports and suppressing imports. Some ways to do accomplish this task have included granting subsidies for exports and imposing tariffs on imports. Mercantilism can be regarded as essentially the opposite of the free trade policies that have been encouraged in more recent years.

44. C: It is not true that the English Civil Wars between 1641 and 1651 legalized Parliament's consent as a requirement for a monarch to rule England. These wars did establish this idea as a precedent, but the later Glorious Revolution of 1688 actually made it legal that a monarch could not rule without Parliamentary consent. The wars from 1641-1651 were all fought between Royalists who supported an absolute monarchy and Parliamentarians who supported the joint government of a parliamentary monarchy (a). Parliament was the victor (b) in 1651 at the Battle of Worcester. As a result of this battle, King Charles I was executed, and King Charles II was exiled. In the first of these civil wars, from 1642-1646, and the second, from 1648-1649, supporters of King Charles I (d) fought against supporters of the Long Parliament. The third, from 1649-1651, involved supporters of King Charles II fighting against supporters of the Rump Parliament.

45. D: Resentment against the Protestant Reformation was not a cause given for the French Revolution. Choices (a), (b), and (c) are just a few among many causes cited for the war. Famines caused malnutrition and even starvation among the poorest people (a). Escalating bread prices contributed greatly to the hunger. Louis XV had amassed a great amount of debt from spending money on many wars in addition to the American Revolution. Military failures as well as a lack of social services for veterans exacerbated these debts. In addition, the Court of Louis XVI and Marie Antoinette spent excessively and obviously on luxuries even while people in the country were starving, and France's monetary system was outdated, inefficient, and thus unable to manage the national debt (b). Much of the populace greatly resented the Catholic Church's control of the country (c). However, there was not great resentment against the Protestant Reformation (d); there were large minorities of Protestants in France, who not only exerted their influence on government institutions, but undoubtedly also contributed to the resentment of the Catholic Church.

46. C: The only accurate statement about the end of WWI is that President Wilson had proposed that the nations of the world form a coalition to prevent future world wars. While he did not give the coalition a name, he clearly expressed his proposal that such a group form in the fourteenth of his Fourteen Points. The Treaty of Versailles (1919) did not bring peace among all countries involved in the war (a); Germany and the United States arrived at a separate peace in 1921. Furthermore, the Treaty of Versailles did not contain a clause for establishing the United Nations (b); it contained a clause for establishing the League of Nations. The League of Nations was created as dictated by the treaty, but when the Second World War proved that this group had failed to prevent future world wars, it was replaced by the United Nations after World War II. President Wilson did not succeed in getting the USA to ratify the League of Nations (d). Although he advocated vigorously for the League of Nations, the U.S. Senate never ratified the proposal. While the USA signed the League of Nations charter, the Senate never ratified it, and the USA never joined the League of Nations.

47. D: All of these empires no longer existed following the armistice ending WWI. The Austro-Hungarian Empire (a), the Ottoman Empire (b), and the German Empire (c) were all among the Central powers that lost the war. As empires capitulated, armistices and peace treaties were signed and the map of Europe was redrawn as territories formerly occupied by Central powers were partitioned. For example, the former Austro-Hungarian Empire was partitioned into Austria, Hungary, Czechoslovakia, Yugoslavia, Transylvania, and Romania. The Treaty of Lausanne (1923) gave Turkey both independence and recognition as successor to the former Ottoman Empire after Turkey refused the earlier Treaty of Sèvres (1920), and Mustafa Kemal Ataturk led the Turkish Independence War. Greece, Bulgaria, and other former Ottoman possessions became independent. The Lausanne Treaty defined the boundaries of these countries as well as the boundaries of Iraq, Syria, Cyprus, Sudan, and Egypt. The Russian Empire was among the Allied powers. Russia not only sustained losses in WWI, but Russia also lost additional numbers in the Russian Revolution of 1917, which destroyed the Empire. Bolsheviks took power in Russia under Lenin and signed the Treaty of Brest-Litovsk with Germany in 1918, thereby formally ending Russia's part in WWI and ending the Eastern Front theatre of the war. The former Russian Empire territories of Latvia, Lithuania, Estonia, Finland, and Poland became independent. Therefore, by the end of the Second World War, these four multinational empires no longer existed.

48. C: It is not true that the Second World War came to be known as "The War to End All Wars." Although this appellation sounds more fitting to WWII, it was actually the description given to the First World War. Of course, at the time of WWI no one knew that WWII would take place, so at that time the phrase seemed a suitable designation. Moreover, world leaders then wanted to avoid another world war in the future and thereby formed the League of Nations to prevent such an occurrence. When this proved unsuccessful in preventing WWII, the United Nations was formed. WWI was the worst war the world had ever experienced at the time, but when WWII broke out, it was far worse than WWI. It is true that in the Second World War, nations mobilized all of their resources—both military and civilian (a), to the point that there was no more distinction between the two. This war also claimed many more civilian casualties and military casualties (b) than previous wars. Very large contributors to the great numbers of civilian casualties were the Holocaust, wherein millions of people including Jews, Catholics, Jehovah's Witnesses, Romani, Poles, Soviet POWs, Freemasons, homosexuals, and people with disabilities were killed. Further, the Second World War was the first war in history to detonate nuclear devices (d), when the United States under President Harry S. Truman bombed Hiroshima and Nagasaki after Japan refused the unconditional surrender terms demanded by the Allies at Potsdam, Germany.

49. D: Japan did not experience more war soon after WWII. Japan not only had good economic recovery from the war as some other nations did; moreover, it experienced tremendous economic growth. Within 40 years of the war's end, Japan boasted one of the world's strongest economies. Greece (a) experienced a civil war from 1946-1949 between the government's army and the Communist Party's army. China (b) went back to the civil war it had been fighting on and off since 1927, resuming the fighting from 1946 until 1950. Korea (c) began the Korean War in 1950 when North Korea invaded South Korea.

50. D: All of these statements are true about post-WWII economic recovery. After the war, the U.S. was responsible for approximately half of the world's industrial production (a). (This statistic decreased by the 1970s.) The economies of West Germany, France, and the Soviet Union all bounced back quickly (b) following the war. Italy's economy was suffering

by the end of the war, but within ten years or less it recovered. China was bankrupt after its Civil War that followed WWII, but within three years, its production had returned to prewar status (c). China's economic growth continued, with one interruption by the failed economic experiment known as the Great Leap Forward; other than this erroneously named economic experiment, the Chinese economy mainly progressed. The United Kingdom's economy was destroyed by the war; unlike the other countries discussed here, it did not recover quickly, but instead went through decades of comparatively lower economic levels than prewar.

51. C: It is not true that the A.C.S. was opposed by most abolitionists for repatriating black people to Africa instead of emancipating them in America. Because slavery was a major economic and social institution in the Southern United States, at this time several decades before the Civil War and the Emancipation Proclamation, most abolitionists actually agreed with and supported the A.C.S.'s activities in repatriating black people to Africa, preferring this action over emancipation. These supporters were against slavery, but they felt black people could enjoy more freedom and equal rights in Africa than in America because of the South's economic dependence on slavery. They included such important politicians as Henry Clay and James Monroe. The A.C.S. helped thousands of (a) slaves to escape to freedom in Africa and (b) free black people to move to Africa where they would not be as disenfranchised as in the United States. It is also true that the A.C.S. founded the African colony of Liberia (d) in 1821 in order to facilitate a free life for repatriating black people.

52. A: The latest occurring decolonization event was the Eastern Bloc and Soviet Satellite states of Armenia, Azerbaijan, Estonia, Georgia, Kazakhstan, Kyrgyzstan, Latvia, Lithuania, Moldova, Russia, Tajikistan, Turkmenistan, Ukraine, and Uzbekistan all became independent from the Soviet Union in 1991. (Note: This was the last decolonization of the Cold War years, as the end of the Soviet Union marked the end of the Cold War.) Canada completed its independence from British Parliament via the Canada Act (b) in 1982. In the Caribbean, the Bahamas gained independence from the United Kingdom (c) in 1973. Algeria won its independence from France when the Algerian War of Independence, begun in 1954, ended in 1962 (d). In Africa, Libya gained independence from Italy and became an independent kingdom in 1951.

53. B: It is not true that the Crusades succeeded at Christians' reclaiming the "holy land" (the Middle East) from Muslims. Despite their number (nine not counting the Northern Crusades) and longevity (1095-1291 not counting later similar campaigns), the Crusades never accomplished this purpose (a). While they did not take back the Middle East, the Crusades did succeed in exacerbating the decline of the Byzantine Empire (c), which lost more and more territory to the Ottoman Turks during this period. In addition, the Crusades resulted in Egypt's rise once again to become a major power (d) of the Middle East as it had been in the past. It is also true that during the Crusades, some Christians and Muslims became allies against common enemies. For example, during the Fifth Crusade, in Anatolia, Christian Crusaders with German, Dutch, Flemish, and Frisian soldiers allied themselves with the Sultanate of Rûm, a Seljuk Turk Sultanate that attacked the Ayyubids in Syria, in order to further their aim of attacking and capturing the port of Damietta in Egypt.

54. C: The New Kingdom was the period during which no more pyramids were built in Egypt. The Pyramids were built between the years of 2630 and 1814 B.C., and the New Kingdom spanned from circa 1550-1070 B.C. As a result, the last pyramid was built approximately 264 years before the New Kingdom began. 2630 B.C. marked the beginning of the reign of the first Pharaoh, Djoser, who had the first pyramid built at Saqqara. 1814

B.C. marked the end of the reign of the last Pharaoh, Amenemhat III, who had the last pyramid built at Hawara. In between these years, a succession of pharaohs built many pyramids. The Old Kingdom (a) encompasses both the Third (d) and Fourth Dynasties; therefore, both choices encompass pyramid-building periods. Djoser's had his first pyramid built during the Third Dynasty (d). The Pharaohs Kufu, Khafre, and Menkaure, respectively, build the famous Pyramids of Giza during the Fourth Dynasty during their reigns at different times between circa 2575 and 2467 B.C., the period of the Fourth Dynasty. The Middle Kingdom (b) encompassed the 11th through 14th Dynasties, from circa. 2080 to 1640 B.C.—also within the time period (2630-1814 B.C.) when pyramids were built by the Pharaohs.

55. D: Federalists who helped frame the Constitution believed the central government needed to be stronger than what was established under the Articles of Confederation. Anti-federalists were against this and feared a strong federal government. A system of checks and balances was established to prevent the central government from taking too much power.

56. C: The Civil Rights Act of 1964 affected the Jim Crowe laws in the Southern states. Many minorities suffered under unfair voting laws and segregation. President Lyndon Johnson signed the Civil Rights Act of 1964 into law after the 1963 assassination of President Kennedy, who championed the reform.

57. B: President John Adams appointed William Marbury as Justice of the Peace, but Secretary of State James Madison never delivered the commission. Marbury claimed that under the Judiciary Act of 1789, the Supreme Court could order his commission be given to him. The Supreme Court denied Marbury's petition citing that the Judiciary Act of 1789 was unconstitutional, although they believed he was entitled to his commission.

58. D: America is a common law country because English common law was adopted in all states except Louisiana. Common law is based on precedent, and changes over time. Each state develops its own common laws.

59. C: The President must be a natural citizen, be at least 35 years old, and have lived in the U.S. for 14 years. There is no education requirement for becoming President. Truman did not have a college education, but most Presidents have degrees.

60. B: The Presidential Succession Act lists the Speaker of the House, President Pro Tempore of the Senate, and Secretary of State next in succession after the Vice President. However, anyone who succeeds as President must meet all of the legal qualifications.

61. C: The President has the power to veto legislation directly or use a pocket veto by not signing a bill within ten days after receiving it. Congress adjourns during this time period. A veto can be overridden if two-thirds of the House and the two-thirds of the Senate both agree. The President must veto a complete bill and does not have the authority to veto sections or lines.

62. D: A member of the House must be at least 25 years old, a U.S. citizen for a minimum of seven years, and a resident of the state he represents. Members of the House do not necessarily need to reside in the districts they represent.

63. B: A Senator must be at least 30 years old, a U.S. citizen for a minimum of nine years, and a resident of the state he represents. Every state elects two Senators, and individual districts are represented in the House of Representatives.

64. D: According to Article III of the Constitution, Justices of the Supreme Court, judges of the courts of appeals and district courts, and judges of the Court of International Trade are appointed by the President with the confirmation of the Senate. The judicial branch of the government is the only one not elected by the people.

65. D: Local governments are usually divided into counties and municipalities. Municipalities oversee parks and recreation services, police and fire departments, housing services, emergency medical services, municipal courts, transportation services, and public works.

66. C: The 12th Amendment passed in 1804 gave each member of the Electoral College one vote for the President and another for the Vice President. Previously, the runner-up in the Presidential election became Vice President.

67. B: Discretionary spending is dedicated to transportation, education, national resources, the environment, and international affairs. State and local governments use this money to help finance programs. Mandatory spending covers entitlements such as Medicare, Social Security, Federal Retirement, and Medicaid.

68. A: The President has the authority to negotiate and sign treaties. Two-thirds vote of the Senate, however, is needed to ratify a treaty for it to be upheld.

69. D: Democratic consensus is the term for the general agreement of the people on fundamental principles of governance and the values supporting them.

70. A: America has a history of organized political protest dating back to the American Revolution. The right to peaceful protest is protected by the First Amendment. The American labor union movement, the antislavery movement, the women's suffrage movement, and the civil rights movement all used political protest to gain support for their causes.

71. A: Compassion issues such as gun control, strong environmental laws, social programs, and opposition to the death penalty show a wide gender gap, as women are more likely to support compassion issues.

72. C: Lobbyists for special interest groups petition the government. Special interest groups have been regulated because of their influence and relationships with members of Congress. PACs and special interest groups are both praised and vilified. The group Common Cause wants to end PACs.

73. A: The UN is a supranational institution made up of participating nations that develop international laws. Recent globalization makes supranational institutions such as the UN, EU, and ECOWAS more influential in political policies.

74. B: Fascism and Marxism both came out of socialism, and while they had some similarities, they did not support each other. Fascism was focused on specific nations, and

Marxism focused on the working class of the world in an attempt to overthrow capitalism. Fascism sought to bring the private sector under government control while preserving private property and class divisions.

75. A: The concept of mixed government dates back to antiquity. Plato and Aristotle both advocated a mixture of monarchic, aristocratic, oligarchic, and democratic governments to prevent a single class, state, or person from taking absolute power. The separation of powers in government preserves the principle of mixed government.

76. B: The International Monetary Fund (IMF) was established in 1944. The IMF works to stabilize foreign trade, reduce trade barriers, and balance trade overall. It has been compared to a credit counselor, but for developing nations. The UNDP provides initiatives and resources to help developing nations.

77. C: A pluralist society is made up of many distinct special interest groups that represent different social minorities. These interest groups compete with each other to influence legislation. The power special interest groups exert is constantly shifting.

78. B: Most political theorists support free international trade. For example, many liberals, Marxists, social democrats, and conservatives support the idea of free international trade; however, most communist regimes have strict trade limitations.

79. B: A bicameral legislature has more than one legislative house, such as an upper house and a lower house. This form of mixed government is supposed to ensure greater representation since it takes both houses to pass legislation. Many authoritarian or communist regimes have unicameral legislature, or one legislative house. Unicameral legislatures do not ensure equal representation, but they pass legislation faster than bicameral legislatures.

80. B: The versions of a bill that pass through both houses of Congress and are signed by the President must have the exact same wording. A conference committee brings the versions of the bill into alignment, but exact wording is rare.

81. A: Presidential candidates are nominated at each party's national convention. The Republican and Democratic Conventions have their own processes for selecting delegates. Puerto Rico, Guam, and American Samoa are also awarded PLEO (Party Leaders and Elected Officials) delegates in the Democratic National Convention.

82. C: The shortest distance between New York and Paris goes over Labrador and Greenland. This is not apparent on a projection map, in which a straight line drawn between the two cities would extend straight out across the Atlantic Ocean, roughly along the 42nd parallel. The illusion that this straight line is the shortest path is a result of the distortions inherent in projection maps. On a globe, it would be easier to see that a plane flying from New York to Paris would cover the least ground by carving an arc, first up through eastern Canada and Greenland and then back down through the British Isles and northern France. This sort of path is known as a great circle route because it looks like an arc when it is drawn on a projection map.

83. B: On a political map, countries are represented in different colors, and countries that share a border are not given the same color. This is so that the borders between countries

will be distinct. Political maps are used to illustrate those aspects of a country that have been determined by people: the capital, the provincial and national borders, and the large cities. Political maps sometimes include major physical features like rivers and mountains, but they are not intended to display all such information. On a physical, climate, or contour map, however, the borders between nations are more incidental. Colors are used on these maps to represent physical features, areas with similar climate, etc. It is possible that colors will overrun the borders and be shared by adjacent countries.

84. A: A smaller box in which some part of the larger map is depicted in greater detail is known as an inset. Insets provide a closer look at parts of the map that the cartographer deems to be more important (for instance, cities, national parks, or historical sites). Often, traffic maps will include several insets depicting the roads in the most congested area of the city. Legends, also known as keys, are the boxes in which the symbols used in the map are explained. A legend, or key, might indicate how railroads and boundaries are depicted, for example. A compass rose indicates how the map is oriented along the north-south axis. It is common for cartographers to tilt a map for ease of display, such that up may not be due north.

85. D: A flow-line map describes the movement of people, trends, or materials across a physical area. The movements depicted on a flow-line map are typically represented by arrows. In more advanced flow-line maps, the width of the arrow corresponds to the quantity of the motion. Flow-line maps usually declare the span of time that is being represented. A political map depicts the man-made aspects of geography, such as borders and cities. A cartogram adjusts the size of the areas represented according to some variable. For instance, a cartogram of wheat production would depict Iowa as being much larger than Alaska. A qualitative map uses lines, dots, and other symbols to illustrate a particular point. For example, a qualitative map might be used to demonstrate the greatest expansion of the Persian Empire.

86. A: Antarctica will appear the largest on a Mercator projection. This projection map converts the globe into a rectangle, such that lines of longitude and latitude are perpendicular to one another. This type of map depicts landforms near the equator at nearly their normal size but increasingly stretches out distances as it reaches the poles. A Robinson projection, on the other hand, rounds the edges of the Mercator projection, such that the polar regions are not so large. A homolosine projection renders the sizes and shapes of landmasses correctly, but it distorts the distances between them. An azimuthal projection represents one hemisphere as a circle, such that a straight line from the center to any point on the map would also be the shortest distance in the real world.

87. C: The cycle of demographic transition is best illustrated by a line graph. Demographic transition is a phenomenon in which a region's growth rate increases rapidly, peaks, and then decreases slowly over a long time. In the early phase of a region's development, both the birth and death rates are high, which can cause the population to fluctuate. As the people of the region become settled, the growth rate calms down, and the region enters a period of rapid increase. Political maps are better at depicting borders and the locations of cities, while pie charts are better at representing proportions. Flow-line maps are good for illustrating the movement of people, goods, or trends across a physical area.

88. A: The eye wall of a hurricane has the strongest winds and the greatest rainfall. The eye wall is the tower-like rim of the eye. It is from this wall that clouds extend out, which are

seen from above as the classic outward spiral pattern. A hurricane front is the outermost edge of its influence; although there will be heavy winds and rain in this area, the intensity will be relatively small. The eye of a hurricane is actually a place of surprising peace. In this area, dry and cool air rushes down to the ground or sea. Once there, the air is caught up in the winds of the eye wall and is driven outward at a furious pace.

89. B: Metamorphic rock is formed by extreme heat and pressure. This type of rock is created when other rocks are somehow buried within the earth, where they are subject to a dramatic rise in pressure and temperature. Slate and marble are both metamorphic rocks. Metamorphic rocks are created by the other two main types of rock: sedimentary and igneous. Sedimentary rock is formed when dirt and other sediment is washed into a bed, covered over by subsequent sediment, and compacted into rock. Depending on how they are formed, sedimentary rocks are classified as organic, clastic, or chemical. Igneous rocks are composed of cooled magma, the molten rock that emerges from volcanoes. Basalt and granite are two common varieties of igneous rock.

90. A: La Niña is a brief interval of coolness in between warm periods (El Niño) in the water of the Pacific Ocean. For a long time, La Niña was considered only in terms of its relation to El Niño. Increasingly, however, it is being studied as a climate event in its own right. A tropical gyre is a circle of winds made up of equatorial currents in one direction and countercurrents in the other direction. There are tropical gyres in both the Northern and Southern hemispheres. El Niño is an annual event, though some years it is considerably more pronounced. It is an increase in the temperature of coastal Pacific water, sometimes by as much as 2° Celsius. El Niño has a great impact on fishing and weather in the areas that border the Pacific Ocean. The El Niño–Southern Oscillation (ENSO) occurs during a particularly intense El Niño; the flow of equatorial wind and water during an ENSO actually reverses course.

91. D: The rocks and land formations that make up the earth's surface are collectively known as the lithosphere. The lithosphere does not include the core or mantle of the earth. The atmosphere is the air, water, and particles that are above the surface of the earth. The biosphere encompasses all the living things of the earth, such as animals, plants, fungi, and bacteria. The hydrosphere is all the water on and beneath the surface of the earth, including all the lakes, oceans, rivers, and creeks.

92. C: In the plate movement known as subduction, an oceanic plate slides underneath a continental plate. Oceanic plates are denser, so they tend to go beneath when they are pressed against lighter continental plates. The edge of the oceanic plate will be melted by the earth's mantle and may reemerge as a volcano. The Cascade Range of the northwest United States was formed by subduction. In faulting, the edges of two plates grind against each other laterally. The San Andreas Fault in California is perhaps the most famous example of this process. In spreading, plates pull apart from each other, typically creating a rift valley and the potential for earthquakes. In converging, two plates of similar density press against each other, creating mountain ranges where they meet.

93. C: Acid rain is an example of chemical weathering. When acidic chemicals are evaporated and fall as rain, they can have devastating effects on plant and animal life. Although human activity is the primary cause of acid rain, weathering chemicals can also get into the atmosphere through oceanic bacteria and volcanoes. The other three answer choices are examples of mechanical weathering. Frost wedging occurs when water seeps

into a narrow space within a rock formation and then freezes. Because water takes up more space as ice and frost than it does in its liquid state, this process can cause structural damage to the rock. Heat expansion occurs when rapid changes in temperature cause rocks to expand, leading to cracks and fissures. Salt wedging occurs when water flowing into a rock brings salt in with it. The water evaporates, but the salt is left behind, and over time the deposits of salt can create pressure within the rock.

94. C: The increasing popularity of Thai food in the United States is an example of cultural convergence, or the intersection of traits or customs from two distinct cultures. Thailand's cuisine has been introduced to the United States, but it has undergone subtle changes as a result of the desires and practices of the American consumer. The phenomenon of cultural convergence is credited with much of the innovation in any society. Cultural divergence, on the other hand, is the practice of shielding one culture from the influence of another. France, for instance, seeks to limit the influence of American culture on its citizens. Assimilation is the process by which a minority group gradually adopts the culture of the majority group. For example, many Native Americans assimilated into the European-style culture of the early American settlers. Acculturation is the process of obtaining the practices and ideas of a culture. A child undergoes acculturation, wherein he or she learns to think and act appropriately for his or her setting.

95. D: Population is not one of the necessary characteristics of a geographical region. A geographical region does not require people. Indeed, such regions as the Hindu Kush or Death Valley have few if any inhabitants. A region does need to have area and location, however. It must be capable of being mapped, and it must be able to be found by travelers. A region also needs homogeneity, which means that it needs some sort of consistent features. It makes sense for a region to include a group of nearby mountains, but it does not make sense for it to include a mountain and an island hundreds of miles away. In human geography, it is necessary for the inhabitants of a region to share some cultural characteristics, such as religion or language.

96. B: Diversity is not one of the demographic variables. Demographers, or those who study population, rely on fertility, mortality, and migration to determine the number of people in a region. The general equation is *Total Population = Original Population + Births – Deaths + Immigration – Emigration*. The natural increase, on the other hand, is calculated only with the number of births and deaths. The diversity of a population may be relevant to subsequent research performed by the demographer, but it is not considered one of the essential three demographic variables.

97. C: The popularity of Japanese anime comics in the United States is an example of indirect diffusion. Indirect cultural diffusion is the spread of ideas or practices from one culture to a distant culture. Indeed, the primary difference between direct and indirect diffusion is distance, or adjacency. Because the United States and Japan are not close to each other, trends that begin in Japan and take root in the United States are examples of indirect diffusion. The Internet has made indirect diffusion a much more common phenomenon.

98. D: When a person grows only enough food to feed himself and his family, he is engaged in subsistence farming. The peasants of undeveloped countries are often forced to rely on subsistence farming because they lack the equipment and water resources to expand their crop. Of course, subsistence farming is not an ideal arrangement because a drought or monsoon can wipe out an entire crop and endanger the lives of the farmers. Nomadic

herding is constant migration accompanied by livestock, particularly cows or sheep. Commercial farming is large scale enough to allow some or all the crops to be sold in a market. Sharecropping is a system wherein a landowner allows tenant farmers to use his or her land in exchange for a portion of the harvest.

99. D: Japan imports the second-highest amount of oil after the United States. Following World War II, Japan rapidly became one of the foremost industrial powers. Despite thriving economically, however, Japan is not especially rich in natural resources. Only slightly more than 10 percent of the nation's land can be farmed, and there are no significant oil deposits. For this reason, Japan must import most of the raw materials it needs for its manufacturing base.

100. B: Dutch is not one of the three official languages in Switzerland, a nation unique in Europe for having several distinct cultures within its borders. The official name of the country is the Swiss Federation. The majority of Swiss speak German, and cities like Zurich and Bern are predominately German in architecture and culture. Geneva, on the other hand, is a largely French-speaking city. There is a local Swiss dialect, known as Romansch, which is spoken by many people despite not being one of the official languages.

101. B: The United States and Canada share the longest undefended border in the world. It is more than 5,000 miles long, stretching from the Atlantic to the Pacific. The fact that there is no fence or military guard on this border is evidence of the strong, friendly bond between these two nations. Indeed, Canada and the United States are also major trading partners. The United States buys about 85 percent of all Canadian exports, and Canada buys about a quarter of everything sold abroad by the United States. There has never been a significant problem with illegal migration between the United States and Canada, though there has been considerable smuggling.

102. A: The production possibilities frontier shows the different possible combinations of goods (and/or services) a society can produce. If all other factors are even, producing more of Good A leads to a decreased production of Good B. If the PPF moves outward, that means a change in the factors of production that allows the economy to produce more goods—economic growth—has occurred. Only Answer A is an example of economic growth.

103. D: Opportunity cost is a measure of what a society gives up to produce a good (or goods). When the society decides to increase its production of Good X from 10 to 15 units, it gives up the ability to produce 4 units of Good Y (with production of Good Y dropping from 10 units to 6 units). The opportunity cost of the decision, then, is 4 units of Good Y.

104. D: Comparative advantage is a measure of the opportunity cost of producing a good. Mexico has an opportunity cost of only 0.5 gallons of oil for each bushel of corn produced (to increase production of corn by 10 bushels, Mexico must decrease oil production by only 5 gallons). Meanwhile, the U.S. has an opportunity cost of 1 gallon of oil for each bushel of corn (to increase production of corn by 20 bushels, the U.S. must decrease oil production by 20 gallons). Mexico has a lower opportunity cost for corn production, therefore

105. A: As people have more and more of something, they value it less and less. This is the law of diminishing marginal utility, and it is what causes the downward slope of the demand curve.

106. C: If the government cuts defense spending but does not shift that money to other spending, that will have a negative effect on AD, causing AD to decrease. All of the other options would increase AD.

107. B: According to the theory of crowding out, when the government borrows money to increase spending, this will increase the price of money, leading to a drop in investment. That drop in investment will have a negative effect on AD, and so the government injection of funds will not have its full, desired effect (AD3), instead winding up at AD2.

108. D: In the long run, aggregate supply does not depend on price. Aggregate supply in the long run depends strictly on the amount of capital and labor and the type of available technology.

109. D: When the FOMC purchases bonds, that brings an increase to the money supply, and there is an increase in bond yields and bond interest rates. When the FOMC sells bonds, that decreases the money supply, and bond yields and bond interest rates go down.

110. D: The opportunity cost of a producer's choice to produce one good is the loss of the ability to use the same resources to produce another good.

111. D: Miguel has a comparative advantage in writing text because he can create 10 pages of text for an opportunity cost of only 1 graphic for a ratio of 10-1, whereas Huan creates 20 pages of text at an opportunity cost of 3 graphics for a ratio of 20-3 or 10-1.5. Miguel's opportunity cost of 1 graphic per 10 pages of text is less than Huan's opportunity cost of 1.5 graphics per 10 pages of text.

112. C: The marginal cost of each pizza is the cost to make that one additional pizza. In this case, the sixth pizza adds only $4 to the total cost, the lowest of all production levels given.

113. C: The production possibilities frontier, or PPF, represents all the possible production combinations of two goods, not all goods. Points inside the frontier are inefficient because they do not fully utilize all available resources. Points on the frontier are efficient because they maximize the usage of all available resources. Points beyond the frontier are unattainable because they offer combinations of goods that are unavailable due to resource and production limitations.

114. C: Because the PPF shows all the combinations of goods that can be produced with a given set of resources, it is bowed, signifying that some combinations of the two goods have different opportunity costs.

115. D: When making an economic decision, the opportunity cost is the lost opportunity to do the next best alternative. Therefore, options a. and c. are incorrect because they define the opportunity cost as the lost option to do two other things. Option b. is incorrect because giving money to charity has an opportunity cost just like spending money does. Option d. is correct because it says the opportunity cost is either purchasing music or donating to charity --- whichever is preferred would be correct but from the question we do not know which is preferred so "or" is appropriate.

116. A: The change in demand is 20% (1,000 – 800 = 200), and the change in price is 10% ($11 - $10 = $1). Because the change in demand is greater than the change in price, the demand is considered elastic. In this case, the price elasticity quotient is greater than 1.

117. D: It is not true that if ES is greater than 1, supply is inelastic. In fact, that is the definition of elastic supply. All the other options are true—a. is another way to define elastic supply, b. is true because the supplier has to sell the goods before they perish, c. is true because production processes are generally fixed in the short run, and d. is true because, given time, a producer can change supply.

118. A: Consumer surplus is the area below the demand curve that is above the equilibrium price line, represented by Area A in this graph.

119. C: If a determinant of demand increases, demand will increase. That means that the demand curve will shift to the right, causing an increase in both the equilibrium price and the equilibrium quantity. An increase in a determinant of demand will not cause any movement to the supply curve.

120. A: Deadweight loss, which is the reduction in efficiency and the decrease in societal welfare, is represented by the area bounded by point A (the original equilibrium price), point B (the price consumers pay for the good), and point C (the price producers receive for the good).

Secret Key #1 - Time is Your Greatest Enemy

Pace Yourself

Wear a watch. At the beginning of the test, check the time (or start a chronometer on your watch to count the minutes), and check the time after every few questions to make sure you are "on schedule." If you are forced to speed up, do it efficiently. Usually one or more answer choices can be eliminated without too much difficulty. Above all, don't panic. Don't speed up and just begin guessing at random choices. By pacing yourself, and continually monitoring your progress against your watch, you will always know exactly how far ahead or behind you are with your available time. If you find that you are one minute behind on the test, don't skip one question without spending any time on it, just to catch back up. Take 15 fewer seconds on the next four questions, and after four questions you'll have caught back up. Once you catch back up, you can continue working each problem at your normal pace.

Furthermore, don't dwell on the problems that you were rushed on. If a problem was taking up too much time and you made a hurried guess, it must be difficult. The difficult questions are the ones you are most likely to miss anyway, so it isn't a big loss. It is better to end with more time than you need than to run out of time.

Lastly, sometimes it is beneficial to slow down if you are constantly getting ahead of time. You are always more likely to catch a careless mistake by working more slowly than quickly, and among very high-scoring test takers (those who are likely to have lots of time left over), careless errors affect the score more than mastery of material.

Secret Key #2 - Guessing is not Guesswork

You probably know that guessing is a good idea. Unlike other standardized tests, there is no penalty for getting a wrong answer. Even if you have no idea about a question, you still have a 20-25% chance of getting it right. Most test takers do not understand the impact that proper guessing can have on their score. Unless you score extremely high, guessing will significantly contribute to your final score.

Monkeys Take the Test

What most test takers don't realize is that to insure that 20-25% chance, you have to guess randomly. If you put 20 monkeys in a room to take this test, assuming they answered once per question and behaved themselves, on average they would get 20-25% of the questions correct. Put 20 test takers in the room, and the average will be much lower among guessed questions. Why?
1. The test writers intentionally write deceptive answer choices that "look" right. A test taker has no idea about a question, so he picks the "best looking" answer, which is often wrong. The monkey has no idea what looks good and what doesn't, so it will consistently be right about 20-25% of the time.
2. Test takers will eliminate answer choices from the guessing pool based on a hunch or intuition. Simple but correct answers often get excluded, leaving a 0% chance of being correct. The monkey has no clue, and often gets lucky with the best choice.

This is why the process of elimination endorsed by most test courses is flawed and detrimental to your performance. Test takers don't guess; they make an ignorant stab in the dark that is usually worse than random.

$5 Challenge

Let me introduce one of the most valuable ideas of this course—the $5 challenge:

- *You only mark your "best guess" if you are willing to bet $5 on it.*
- *You only eliminate choices from guessing if you are willing to bet $5 on it.*

Why $5? Five dollars is an amount of money that is small yet not insignificant, and can really add up fast (20 questions could cost you $100). Likewise, each answer choice on one question of the test will have a small impact on your overall score, but it can really add up to a lot of points in the end.

The process of elimination IS valuable. The following shows your chance of guessing it right:

If you eliminate wrong answer choices until only this many remain:	Chance of getting it correct:
1	100%
2	50%
3	33%

However, if you accidentally eliminate the right answer or go on a hunch for an incorrect answer, your chances drop dramatically—to 0%. By guessing among all the answer choices, you are GUARANTEED to have a shot at the right answer. That's why the $5 test is so valuable. If you give up the advantage and safety of a pure guess, it had better be worth the risk.

What we still haven't covered is how to be sure that whatever guess you make is truly random. Here's the easiest way:

- *Always pick the first answer choice among those remaining.*

Such a technique means that you have decided, **before you see a single test question**, exactly how you are going to guess, and since the order of choices tells you nothing about which one is correct, this guessing technique is perfectly random.

This section is not meant to scare you away from making educated guesses or eliminating choices; you just need to define when a choice is worth eliminating. The $5 test, along with a pre-defined random guessing strategy, is the best way to make sure you reap all of the benefits of guessing.

Secret Key #3 - Practice Smarter, Not Harder

Many test takers delay the test preparation process because they dread the awful amounts of practice time they think necessary to succeed on the test. We have refined an effective method that will take you only a fraction of the time.

There are a number of "obstacles" in the path to success. Among these are answering questions, finishing in time, and mastering test-taking strategies. All must be executed on the day of the test at peak performance, or your score will suffer. The test is a mental marathon that has a large impact on your future.

Just like a marathon runner, it is important to work your way up to the full challenge. So first you just worry about questions, and then time, and finally strategy:

Success Strategy

1. Find a good source for practice tests.
2. If you are willing to make a larger time investment, consider using more than one study guide. Often the different approaches of multiple authors will help you "get" difficult concepts.
3. Take a practice test with no time constraints, with all study helps, "open book." Take your time with questions and focus on applying strategies.
4. Take a practice test with time constraints, with all guides, "open book."
5. Take a final practice test without open material and with time limits.

If you have time to take more practice tests, just repeat step 5. By gradually exposing yourself to the full rigors of the test environment, you will condition your mind to the stress of test day and maximize your success.

Secret Key #4 - Prepare, Don't Procrastinate

Let me state an obvious fact: if you take the test three times, you will probably get three different scores. This is due to the way you feel on test day, the level of preparedness you have, and the version of the test you see. Despite the test writers' claims to the contrary, some versions of the test WILL be easier for you than others.

Since your future depends so much on your score, you should maximize your chances of success. In order to maximize the likelihood of success, you've got to prepare in advance. This means taking practice tests and spending time learning the information and test taking strategies you will need to succeed.

Never go take the actual test as a "practice" test, expecting that you can just take it again if you need to. Take all the practice tests you can on your own, but when you go to take the official test, be prepared, be focused, and do your best the first time!

Secret Key #5 - Test Yourself

Everyone knows that time is money. There is no need to spend too much of your time or too little of your time preparing for the test. You should only spend as much of your precious time preparing as is necessary for you to get the score you need.

Once you have taken a practice test under real conditions of time constraints, then you will know if you are ready for the test or not.

If you have scored extremely high the first time that you take the practice test, then there is not much point in spending countless hours studying. You are already there.

Benchmark your abilities by retaking practice tests and seeing how much you have improved. Once you consistently score high enough to guarantee success, then you are ready.

If you have scored well below where you need, then knuckle down and begin studying in earnest. Check your improvement regularly through the use of practice tests under real conditions. Above all, don't worry, panic, or give up. The key is perseverance!

Then, when you go to take the test, remain confident and remember how well you did on the practice tests. If you can score high enough on a practice test, then you can do the same on the real thing.

General Strategies

The most important thing you can do is to ignore your fears and jump into the test immediately. Do not be overwhelmed by any strange-sounding terms. You have to jump into the test like jumping into a pool—all at once is the easiest way.

Make Predictions

As you read and understand the question, try to guess what the answer will be. Remember that several of the answer choices are wrong, and once you begin reading them, your mind will immediately become cluttered with answer choices designed to throw you off. Your mind is typically the most focused immediately after you have read the question and digested its contents. If you can, try to predict what the correct answer will be. You may be surprised at what you can predict. Quickly scan the choices and see if your prediction is in the listed answer choices. If it is, then you can be quite confident that you have the right answer. It still won't hurt to check the other answer choices, but most of the time, you've got it!

Answer the Question

It may seem obvious to only pick answer choices that answer the question, but the test writers can create some excellent answer choices that are wrong. Don't pick an answer just because it sounds right, or you believe it to be true. It MUST answer the question. Once you've made your selection, always go back and check it against the question and make sure that you didn't misread the question and that the answer choice does answer the question posed.

Benchmark

After you read the first answer choice, decide if you think it sounds correct or not. If it doesn't, move on to the next answer choice. If it does, mentally mark that answer choice. This doesn't mean that you've definitely selected it as your answer choice, it just means that it's the best you've seen thus far. Go ahead and read the next choice. If the next choice is worse than the one you've already selected, keep going to the next answer choice. If the next choice is better than the choice you've already selected, mentally mark the new answer choice as your best guess.

The first answer choice that you select becomes your standard. Every other answer choice must be benchmarked against that standard. That choice is correct until proven otherwise by another answer choice beating it out. Once you've decided that no other answer choice seems as good, do one final check to ensure that your answer choice answers the question posed.

Valid Information

Don't discount any of the information provided in the question. Every piece of information may be necessary to determine the correct answer. None of the information in the question is there to throw you off (while the answer choices will certainly have information to throw you off). If two seemingly unrelated topics are discussed, don't ignore either. You can be confident there is a relationship, or it wouldn't be included in the question, and you are probably going to have to determine what is that relationship to find the answer.

Avoid "Fact Traps"

Don't get distracted by a choice that is factually true. Your search is for the answer that answers the question. Stay focused and don't fall for an answer that is true but irrelevant. Always go back to the question and make sure you're choosing an answer that actually answers the question and is not just a true statement. An answer can be factually correct, but it MUST answer the question asked. Additionally, two answers can both be seemingly correct, so be sure to read all of the answer choices, and make sure that you get the one that BEST answers the question.

Milk the Question

Some of the questions may throw you completely off. They might deal with a subject you have not been exposed to, or one that you haven't reviewed in years. While your lack of knowledge about the subject will be a hindrance, the question itself can give you many clues that will help you find the correct answer. Read the question carefully and look for clues. Watch particularly for adjectives and nouns describing difficult terms or words that you don't recognize. Regardless of whether you completely understand a word or not, replacing it with a synonym, either provided or one you more familiar with, may help you to understand what the questions are asking. Rather than wracking your mind about specific detailed information concerning a difficult term or word, try to use mental substitutes that are easier to understand.

The Trap of Familiarity

Don't just choose a word because you recognize it. On difficult questions, you may not recognize a number of words in the answer choices. The test writers don't put "make-believe" words on the test, so don't think that just because you only recognize all the words in one answer choice that that answer choice must be correct. If you only recognize words in one answer choice, then focus on that one. Is it correct? Try your best to determine if it is correct. If it is, that's great. If not, eliminate it. Each word and answer choice you eliminate increases your chances of getting the question correct, even if you then have to guess among the unfamiliar choices.

Eliminate Answers

Eliminate choices as soon as you realize they are wrong. But be careful! Make sure you consider all of the possible answer choices. Just because one appears right, doesn't mean that the next one won't be even better! The test writers will usually put more than one good answer choice for every question, so read all of them. Don't worry if you are stuck between two that seem right. By getting down to just two remaining possible choices, your odds are now 50/50. Rather than wasting too much time, play the odds. You are guessing, but guessing wisely because you've been able to knock out some of the answer choices that you know are wrong. If you are eliminating choices and realize that the last answer choice you are left with is also obviously wrong, don't panic. Start over and consider each choice again. There may easily be something that you missed the first time and will realize on the second pass.

Tough Questions

If you are stumped on a problem or it appears too hard or too difficult, don't waste time. Move on! Remember though, if you can quickly check for obviously incorrect answer choices, your chances of guessing correctly are greatly improved. Before you completely give up, at least try to knock out a couple of possible answers. Eliminate what you can and then guess at the remaining answer choices before moving on.

Brainstorm

If you get stuck on a difficult question, spend a few seconds quickly brainstorming. Run through the complete list of possible answer choices. Look at each choice and ask yourself, "Could this answer the question satisfactorily?" Go through each answer choice and consider it independently of the others. By systematically going through all possibilities, you may find something that you would otherwise overlook. Remember though that when you get stuck, it's important to try to keep moving.

Read Carefully

Understand the problem. Read the question and answer choices carefully. Don't miss the question because you misread the terms. You have plenty of time to read each question thoroughly and make sure you understand what is being asked. Yet a happy medium must be attained, so don't waste too much time. You must read carefully, but efficiently.

Face Value

When in doubt, use common sense. Always accept the situation in the problem at face value. Don't read too much into it. These problems will not require you to make huge leaps of logic. The test writers aren't trying to throw you off with a cheap trick. If you have to go beyond creativity and make a leap of logic in order to have an answer choice answer the question, then you should look at the other answer choices. Don't overcomplicate the problem by creating theoretical relationships or explanations that will warp time or space. These are normal problems rooted in reality. It's just that the applicable relationship or explanation may not be readily apparent and you have to figure things out. Use your common sense to interpret anything that isn't clear.

Prefixes

If you're having trouble with a word in the question or answer choices, try dissecting it. Take advantage of every clue that the word might include. Prefixes and suffixes can be a huge help. Usually they allow you to determine a basic meaning. Pre- means before, post- means after, pro - is positive, de- is negative. From these prefixes and suffixes, you can get an idea of the general meaning of the word and try to put it into context. Beware though of any traps. Just because con- is the opposite of pro-, doesn't necessarily mean congress is the opposite of progress!

Hedge Phrases

Watch out for critical hedge phrases, led off with words such as "likely," "may," "can," "sometimes," "often," "almost," "mostly," "usually," "generally," "rarely," and "sometimes." Question writers insert these hedge phrases to cover every possibility. Often an answer choice will be wrong simply because it leaves no room for exception. Unless the situation calls for them, avoid answer choices that have definitive words like "exactly," and "always."

Switchback Words

Stay alert for "switchbacks." These are the words and phrases frequently used to alert you to shifts in thought. The most common switchback word is "but." Others include "although," "however," "nevertheless," "on the other hand," "even though," "while," "in spite of," "despite," and "regardless of."

New Information

Correct answer choices will rarely have completely new information included. Answer choices typically are straightforward reflections of the material asked about and will directly relate to the question. If a new piece of information is included in an answer choice that doesn't even seem to relate to the topic being asked about, then that answer choice is likely incorrect. All of the information needed to answer the question is usually provided for you in the question. You should not have to make guesses that are unsupported or choose answer choices that require unknown information that cannot be reasoned from what is given.

Time Management

On technical questions, don't get lost on the technical terms. Don't spend too much time on any one question. If you don't know what a term means, then odds are you aren't going to get much further since you don't have a dictionary. You should be able to immediately recognize whether or not you know a term. If you don't, work with the other clues that you have—the other answer choices and terms provided—but don't waste too much time trying to figure out a difficult term that you don't know.

Contextual Clues

Look for contextual clues. An answer can be right but not the correct answer. The contextual clues will help you find the answer that is most right and is correct. Understand the context in which a phrase or statement is made. This will help you make important distinctions.

Don't Panic

Panicking will not answer any questions for you; therefore, it isn't helpful. When you first see the question, if your mind goes blank, take a deep breath. Force yourself to mechanically go through the steps of solving the problem using the strategies you've learned.

Pace Yourself

Don't get clock fever. It's easy to be overwhelmed when you're looking at a page full of questions, your mind is full of random thoughts and feeling confused, and the clock is ticking down faster than you would like. Calm down and maintain the pace that you have set for yourself. As long as you are on track by monitoring your pace, you are guaranteed to have enough time for yourself. When you get to the last few minutes of the test, it may seem like you won't have enough time left, but if you only have as many questions as you should have left at that point, then you're right on track!

Answer Selection

The best way to pick an answer choice is to eliminate all of those that are wrong, until only one is left and confirm that is the correct answer. Sometimes though, an answer choice may immediately look right. Be careful! Take a second to make sure that the other choices are not equally obvious. Don't make a hasty mistake. There are only two times that you should stop before checking other answers. First is when you are positive that the answer choice you have selected is correct. Second is when time is almost out and you have to make a quick guess!

Check Your Work

Since you will probably not know every term listed and the answer to every question, it is important that you get credit for the ones that you do know. Don't miss any questions through careless mistakes. If at all possible, try to take a second to look back over your answer selection and make sure you've selected the correct answer choice and haven't made a costly careless mistake (such as marking an answer choice that you didn't mean to mark). The time it takes for this quick double check should more than pay for itself in caught mistakes.

Beware of Directly Quoted Answers

Sometimes an answer choice will repeat word for word a portion of the question or reference section. However, beware of such exact duplication. It may be a trap! More than likely, the correct choice will paraphrase or summarize a point, rather than being exactly the same wording.

Slang

Scientific sounding answers are better than slang ones. An answer choice that begins "To compare the outcomes..." is much more likely to be correct than one that begins "Because some people insisted..."

Extreme Statements

Avoid wild answers that throw out highly controversial ideas that are proclaimed as established fact. An answer choice that states the "process should used in certain situations, if..." is much more likely to be correct than one that states the "process should be discontinued completely." The first is a calm rational statement and doesn't even make a definitive, uncompromising stance, using a hedge word "if" to provide wiggle room, whereas the second choice is a radical idea and far more extreme.

Answer Choice Families

When you have two or more answer choices that are direct opposites or parallels, one of them is usually the correct answer. For instance, if one answer choice states "x increases" and another answer choice states "x decreases" or "y increases," then those two or three answer choices are very similar in construction and fall into the same family of answer choices. A family of answer choices consists of two or three answer choices, very similar in construction, but often with directly opposite meanings. Usually the correct answer choice will be in that family of answer choices. The "odd man out" or answer choice that doesn't seem to fit the parallel construction of the other answer choices is more likely to be incorrect.

Special Report: How to Overcome Test Anxiety

The very nature of tests caters to some level of anxiety, nervousness, or tension, just as we feel for any important event that occurs in our lives. A little bit of anxiety or nervousness can be a good thing. It helps us with motivation, and makes achievement just that much sweeter. However, too much anxiety can be a problem, especially if it hinders our ability to function and perform.

"Test anxiety," is the term that refers to the emotional reactions that some test-takers experience when faced with a test or exam. Having a fear of testing and exams is based upon a rational fear, since the test-taker's performance can shape the course of an academic career. Nevertheless, experiencing excessive fear of examinations will only interfere with the test-taker's ability to perform and chance to be successful.

There are a large variety of causes that can contribute to the development and sensation of test anxiety. These include, but are not limited to, lack of preparation and worrying about issues surrounding the test.

Lack of Preparation

Lack of preparation can be identified by the following behaviors or situations:
- Not scheduling enough time to study, and therefore cramming the night before the test or exam
- Managing time poorly, to create the sensation that there is not enough time to do everything
- Failing to organize the text information in advance, so that the study material consists of the entire text and not simply the pertinent information
- Poor overall studying habits

Worrying, on the other hand, can be related to both the test taker, or many other factors around him/her that will be affected by the results of the test. These include worrying about:
- Previous performances on similar exams, or exams in general
- How friends and other students are achieving
- The negative consequences that will result from a poor grade or failure

There are three primary elements to test anxiety. Physical components, which involve the same typical bodily reactions as those to acute anxiety (to be discussed below). Emotional factors have to do with fear or panic. Mental or cognitive issues concerning attention spans and memory abilities.

Physical Signals

There are many different symptoms of test anxiety, and these are not limited to mental and emotional strain. Frequently there are a range of physical signals that will let a test taker know that he/she is suffering from test anxiety. These bodily changes can include the following:

- Perspiring
- Sweaty palms
- Wet, trembling hands
- Nausea
- Dry mouth
- A knot in the stomach
- Headache
- Faintness
- Muscle tension
- Aching shoulders, back and neck
- Rapid heart beat
- Feeling too hot/cold

To recognize the sensation of test anxiety, a test-taker should monitor him/herself for the following sensations:

- The physical distress symptoms as listed above
- Emotional sensitivity, expressing emotional feelings such as the need to cry or laugh too much, or a sensation of anger or helplessness
- A decreased ability to think, causing the test-taker to blank out or have racing thoughts that are hard to organize or control

Though most students will feel some level of anxiety when faced with a test or exam, the majority can cope with that anxiety and maintain it at a manageable level. However, those who cannot are faced with a very real and very serious condition, which can and should be controlled for the immeasurable benefit of this sufferer. Naturally, these sensations lead to negative results for the testing experience. The most common effects of test anxiety have to do with nervousness and mental blocking.

Nervousness

Nervousness can appear in several different levels:

- The test-taker's difficulty, or even inability to read and understand the questions on the test
- The difficulty or inability to organize thoughts to a coherent form
- The difficulty or inability to recall key words and concepts relating to the testing questions (especially essays)
- The receipt of poor grades on a test, though the test material was well known by the test taker

Conversely, a person may also experience mental blocking, which involves:

- Blanking out on test questions
- Only remembering the correct answers to the questions when the test has already finished

Fortunately for test anxiety sufferers, beating these feelings, to a large degree, has to do with proper preparation. When a test taker has a feeling of preparedness, then anxiety will be dramatically lessened.

The first step to resolving anxiety issues is to distinguish which of the two types of anxiety are being suffered. If the anxiety is a direct result of a lack of preparation, this should be considered a normal reaction, and the anxiety level (as opposed to the test results) shouldn't be anything to worry about. However, if, when adequately prepared, the test-taker still panics, blanks out, or seems to overreact, this is not a fully rational reaction. While this can be considered normal too, there are many ways to combat and overcome these effects.

Remember that anxiety cannot be entirely eliminated, however, there are ways to minimize it, to make the anxiety easier to manage. Preparation is one of the best ways to minimize test anxiety. Therefore the following techniques are wise in order to best fight off any anxiety that may want to build.

To begin with, try to avoid cramming before a test, whenever it is possible. By trying to memorize an entire term's worth of information in one day, you'll be shocking your system, and not giving yourself a very good chance to absorb the information. This is an easy path to anxiety, so for those who suffer from test anxiety, cramming should not even be considered an option.

Instead of cramming, work throughout the semester to combine all of the material which is presented throughout the semester, and work on it gradually as the course goes by, making sure to master the main concepts first, leaving minor details for a week or so before the test.

To study for the upcoming exam, be sure to pose questions that may be on the examination, to gauge the ability to answer them by integrating the ideas from your texts, notes and lectures, as well as any supplementary readings.

If it is truly impossible to cover all of the information that was covered in that particular term, concentrate on the most important portions, that can be covered very well. Learn these concepts as best as possible, so that when the test comes, a goal can be made to use these concepts as presentations of your knowledge.

In addition to study habits, changes in attitude are critical to beating a struggle with test anxiety. In fact, an improvement of the perspective over the entire test-taking experience can actually help a test taker to enjoy studying and therefore improve the overall experience. Be certain not to overemphasize the significance of the grade - know that the result of the test is neither a reflection of self worth, nor is it a measure of intelligence; one grade will not predict a person's future success.

To improve an overall testing outlook, the following steps should be tried:
- Keeping in mind that the most reasonable expectation for taking a test is to expect to try to demonstrate as much of what you know as you possibly can.
- Reminding ourselves that a test is only one test; this is not the only one, and there will be others.

- The thought of thinking of oneself in an irrational, all-or-nothing term should be avoided at all costs.
- A reward should be designated for after the test, so there's something to look forward to. Whether it be going to a movie, going out to eat, or simply visiting friends, schedule it in advance, and do it no matter what result is expected on the exam.

Test-takers should also keep in mind that the basics are some of the most important things, even beyond anti-anxiety techniques and studying. Never neglect the basic social, emotional and biological needs, in order to try to absorb information. In order to best achieve, these three factors must be held as just as important as the studying itself.

Study Steps

Remember the following important steps for studying:
- Maintain healthy nutrition and exercise habits. Continue both your recreational activities and social pass times. These both contribute to your physical and emotional well being.
- Be certain to get a good amount of sleep, especially the night before the test, because when you're overtired you are not able to perform to the best of your best ability.
- Keep the studying pace to a moderate level by taking breaks when they are needed, and varying the work whenever possible, to keep the mind fresh instead of getting bored.
- When enough studying has been done that all the material that can be learned has been learned, and the test taker is prepared for the test, stop studying and do something relaxing such as listening to music, watching a movie, or taking a warm bubble bath.

There are also many other techniques to minimize the uneasiness or apprehension that is experienced along with test anxiety before, during, or even after the examination. In fact, there are a great deal of things that can be done to stop anxiety from interfering with lifestyle and performance. Again, remember that anxiety will not be eliminated entirely, and it shouldn't be. Otherwise that "up" feeling for exams would not exist, and most of us depend on that sensation to perform better than usual. However, this anxiety has to be at a level that is manageable.

Of course, as we have just discussed, being prepared for the exam is half the battle right away. Attending all classes, finding out what knowledge will be expected on the exam, and knowing the exam schedules are easy steps to lowering anxiety. Keeping up with work will remove the need to cram, and efficient study habits will eliminate wasted time. Studying should be done in an ideal location for concentration, so that it is simple to become interested in the material and give it complete attention.
A method such as SQ3R (Survey, Question, Read, Recite, Review) is a wonderful key to follow to make sure that the study habits are as effective as possible, especially in the case of learning from a textbook. Flashcards are great techniques for memorization. Learning to take good notes will mean that notes will be full of useful information, so that less sifting will need to be done to seek out what is pertinent for studying.

Reviewing notes after class and then again on occasion will keep the information fresh in the mind. From notes that have been taken summary sheets and outlines can be made for simpler reviewing.

A study group can also be a very motivational and helpful place to study, as there will be a sharing of ideas, all of the minds can work together, to make sure that everyone understands, and the studying will be made more interesting because it will be a social occasion. Basically, though, as long as the test-taker remains organized and self confident, with efficient study habits, less time will need to be spent studying, and higher grades will be achieved.

To become self confident, there are many useful steps. The first of these is "self talk." It has been shown through extensive research, that self-talk for students who suffer from test anxiety, should be well monitored, in order to make sure that it contributes to self confidence as opposed to sinking the student. Frequently the self talk of test-anxious students is negative or self-defeating, thinking that everyone else is smarter and faster, that they always mess up, and that if they don't do well, they'll fail the entire course. It is important to decreasing anxiety that awareness is made of self talk. Try writing any negative self thoughts and then disputing them with a positive statement instead. Begin self-encouragement as though it was a friend speaking. Repeat positive statements to help reprogram the mind to believing in successes instead of failures.

Helpful Techniques

Other extremely helpful techniques include:
- Self-visualization of doing well and reaching goals
- While aiming for an "A" level of understanding, don't try to "overprotect" by setting your expectations lower. This will only convince the mind to stop studying in order to meet the lower expectations.
- Don't make comparisons with the results or habits of other students. These are individual factors, and different things work for different people, causing different results.
- Strive to become an expert in learning what works well, and what can be done in order to improve. Consider collecting this data in a journal.
- Create rewards for after studying instead of doing things before studying that will only turn into avoidance behaviors.
- Make a practice of relaxing - by using methods such as progressive relaxation, self-hypnosis, guided imagery, etc - in order to make relaxation an automatic sensation.
- Work on creating a state of relaxed concentration so that concentrating will take on the focus of the mind, so that none will be wasted on worrying.
- Take good care of the physical self by eating well and getting enough sleep.
- Plan in time for exercise and stick to this plan.

Beyond these techniques, there are other methods to be used before, during and after the test that will help the test-taker perform well in addition to overcoming anxiety.

Before the exam comes the academic preparation. This involves establishing a study schedule and beginning at least one week before the actual date of the test. By doing this, the anxiety of not having enough time to study for the test will be automatically eliminated. Moreover, this will make the studying a much more effective experience, ensuring that the learning will be an easier process. This relieves much undue pressure on the test-taker.

Summary sheets, note cards, and flash cards with the main concepts and examples of these main concepts should be prepared in advance of the actual studying time. A topic should never be eliminated from this process. By omitting a topic because it isn't expected to be on the test is only setting up the test-taker for anxiety should it actually appear on the exam. Utilize the course syllabus for laying out the topics that should be studied. Carefully go over the notes that were made in class, paying special attention to any of the issues that the professor took special care to emphasize while lecturing in class. In the textbooks, use the chapter review, or if possible, the chapter tests, to begin your review.

It may even be possible to ask the instructor what information will be covered on the exam, or what the format of the exam will be (for example, multiple choice, essay, free form, true-false). Additionally, see if it is possible to find out how many questions will be on the test. If a review sheet or sample test has been offered by the professor, make good use of it, above anything else, for the preparation for the test. Another great resource for getting to know the examination is reviewing tests from previous semesters. Use these tests to review, and aim to achieve a 100% score on each of the possible topics. With a few exceptions, the goal that you set for yourself is the highest one that you will reach.

Take all of the questions that were assigned as homework, and rework them to any other possible course material. The more problems reworked, the more skill and confidence will form as a result. When forming the solution to a problem, write out each of the steps. Don't simply do head work. By doing as many steps on paper as possible, much clarification and therefore confidence will be formed. Do this with as many homework problems as possible, before checking the answers. By checking the answer after each problem, a reinforcement will exist, that will not be on the exam. Study situations should be as exam-like as possible, to prime the test-taker's system for the experience. By waiting to check the answers at the end, a psychological advantage will be formed, to decrease the stress factor.

Another fantastic reason for not cramming is the avoidance of confusion in concepts, especially when it comes to mathematics. 8-10 hours of study will become one hundred percent more effective if it is spread out over a week or at least several days, instead of doing it all in one sitting. Recognize that the human brain requires time in order to assimilate new material, so frequent breaks and a span of study time over several days will be much more beneficial.

Additionally, don't study right up until the point of the exam. Studying should stop a minimum of one hour before the exam begins. This allows the brain to rest and put things in their proper order. This will also provide the time to become as relaxed as possible when going into the examination room. The test-taker will also have time to eat well and eat sensibly. Know that the brain needs food as much as the rest of the body. With enough food and enough sleep, as well as a relaxed attitude, the body and the mind are primed for success.

Avoid any anxious classmates who are talking about the exam. These students only spread anxiety, and are not worth sharing the anxious sentimentalities.

Before the test also involves creating a positive attitude, so mental preparation should also be a point of concentration. There are many keys to creating a positive attitude. Should fears become rushing in, make a visualization of taking the exam, doing well, and seeing an A written on the paper. Write out a list of affirmations that will bring a feeling of confidence, such as "I am doing well in my English class," "I studied well and know my material," "I enjoy this class." Even if the affirmations aren't believed at first, it sends a positive message to the subconscious which will result in an alteration of the overall belief system, which is the system that creates reality.

If a sensation of panic begins, work with the fear and imagine the very worst! Work through the entire scenario of not passing the test, failing the entire course, and dropping out of school, followed by not getting a job, and pushing a shopping cart through the dark alley where you'll live. This will place things into perspective! Then, practice deep breathing and create a visualization of the opposite situation - achieving an "A" on the exam, passing the entire course, receiving the degree at a graduation ceremony.

On the day of the test, there are many things to be done to ensure the best results, as well as the most calm outlook. The following stages are suggested in order to maximize test-taking potential:
- Begin the examination day with a moderate breakfast, and avoid any coffee or beverages with caffeine if the test taker is prone to jitters. Even people who are used to managing caffeine can feel jittery or light-headed when it is taken on a test day.
- Attempt to do something that is relaxing before the examination begins. As last minute cramming clouds the mastering of overall concepts, it is better to use this time to create a calming outlook.
- Be certain to arrive at the test location well in advance, in order to provide time to select a location that is away from doors, windows and other distractions, as well as giving enough time to relax before the test begins.
- Keep away from anxiety generating classmates who will upset the sensation of stability and relaxation that is being attempted before the exam.
- Should the waiting period before the exam begins cause anxiety, create a self-distraction by reading a light magazine or something else that is relaxing and simple.

During the exam itself, read the entire exam from beginning to end, and find out how much time should be allotted to each individual problem. Once writing the exam, should more time be taken for a problem, it should be abandoned, in order to begin another problem. If there is time at the end, the unfinished problem can always be returned to and completed.

Read the instructions very carefully - twice - so that unpleasant surprises won't follow during or after the exam has ended.

When writing the exam, pretend that the situation is actually simply the completion of homework within a library, or at home. This will assist in forming a relaxed atmosphere, and will allow the brain extra focus for the complex thinking function.

Begin the exam with all of the questions with which the most confidence is felt. This will build the confidence level regarding the entire exam and will begin a quality momentum. This will also create encouragement for trying the problems where uncertainty resides.

Going with the "gut instinct" is always the way to go when solving a problem. Second guessing should be avoided at all costs. Have confidence in the ability to do well.

For essay questions, create an outline in advance that will keep the mind organized and make certain that all of the points are remembered. For multiple choice, read every answer, even if the correct one has been spotted - a better one may exist.

Continue at a pace that is reasonable and not rushed, in order to be able to work carefully. Provide enough time to go over the answers at the end, to check for small errors that can be corrected.

Should a feeling of panic begin, breathe deeply, and think of the feeling of the body releasing sand through its pores. Visualize a calm, peaceful place, and include all of the sights, sounds and sensations of this image. Continue the deep breathing, and take a few minutes to continue this with closed eyes. When all is well again, return to the test.

If a "blanking" occurs for a certain question, skip it and move on to the next question. There will be time to return to the other question later. Get everything done that can be done, first, to guarantee all the grades that can be compiled, and to build all of the confidence possible. Then return to the weaker questions to build the marks from there.

Remember, one's own reality can be created, so as long as the belief is there, success will follow. And remember: anxiety can happen later, right now, there's an exam to be written!

After the examination is complete, whether there is a feeling for a good grade or a bad grade, don't dwell on the exam, and be certain to follow through on the reward that was promised...and enjoy it! Don't dwell on any mistakes that have been made, as there is nothing that can be done at this point anyway.

Additionally, don't begin to study for the next test right away. Do something relaxing for a while, and let the mind relax and prepare itself to begin absorbing information again.

From the results of the exam - both the grade and the entire experience, be certain to learn from what has gone on. Perfect studying habits and work some more on confidence in order to make the next examination experience even better than the last one.

Learn to avoid places where openings occurred for laziness, procrastination and day dreaming.

Use the time between this exam and the next one to better learn to relax, even learning to relax on cue, so that any anxiety can be controlled during the next exam. Learn how to relax the body. Slouch in your chair if that helps. Tighten and then relax all of the different muscle groups, one group at a time, beginning with the feet and then working all the way up to the neck and face. This will ultimately relax the muscles more than they were to begin with. Learn how to breathe deeply and comfortably, and focus on this breathing going in and out as a relaxing thought. With every exhale, repeat the word "relax."

As common as test anxiety is, it is very possible to overcome it. Make yourself one of the test-takers who overcome this frustrating hindrance.

Additional Bonus Material

Due to our efforts to try to keep this book to a manageable length, we've created a link that will give you access to all of your additional bonus material.

Please visit http://www.mometrix.com/bonus948/priicitedck to access the information.